It Began Before Noah

Also by Doris Rybot

Non-fiction

MY KINGDOM FOR A DONKEY (Hutchinson)
A DONKEY AND A DANDELION (Hutchinson)

Fiction

ROMANY SISTER (Robert Hale)
A JAPANESE DOLL (Robert Hale)

It Began Before Noah

Doris Rybot

London

Michael Joseph

First published in Great Britain
by Michael Joseph Ltd
52 Bedford Square, London, W.C.I.
1972

7181 0973 2
Printed in the German Democratic Republic by
Offizin Andersen Nexö, Leipzig

TO JOHN

Acknowledgements

I wish to record my very grateful thanks to Mr R. E. Greed, Director of the Bristol Zoo, and to his son, Mr. Geoffrey Greed, for their kindness in answering diverse questions and, while doing so, adding other relevant information; also for providing "diet sheets" for lion, elephant and rhinoceros. No one could have been more helpful.

Also thanks are due to Mr Jonathan Shepard for drawing my attention to the mechanical lions described by Bishop Liudprand in the 10th century: but for him I should have overlooked these.

D.R.

Contents

CHAPTER I

The Lost Skill

The original theme of this book was to explore Man's association with wild animals: how he has kept them, abused them, admired them, even worshipped them. Inevitably, it has turned into a history of early zoos; or if history, given the limited space at my command, is too grand a word, let us say an outline. I have purposely stopped short on the threshold of the 20th century; for there are books enough on modern zoos, animal parks, circuses and the rest.

It can, however, be mentioned in passing that the present-day collections of wild animals made by our aristocracy—such as at Woburn and Longleat—are very far from being a novelty. Over millennia great men have kept wild animals. What *is* new is the situation that, whereas in earlier ages these beasts were kept for the nobleman's own prestige, pleasure and amusement, now circumstances have forced him to become an earner, and his parks are there quite simply to make money. Woburn, to be sure, is in a slightly different category; for the Dukes of Bedford housed exotic animals long before it became necessary for them to put them on show.

Of course all animals were wild once; but I am not penetrating so far back as to a time when the first wolf-cub was scruffed into the cave and (probably) the woman or the child begged his life to be spared; or even when the first ass carried a burden before Abraham. No one knows at what period of history the first creature was brought under the yoke of Man. It is generally conceded that the first species was the wolf or jackal, animals from which spring all our race of dogs. Then, from beyond our knowledge, the goat, or cow, for their milk; the sheep for its meat and wool; the ass or camel to carry a load. In what order is of little consequence. What we certainly know is that all these animals were domestic thousands of years before Christ was born. This is a fact that can scarcely be overstressed.

For it is curious indeed that mankind, who has advanced immeasurably in science, arts and other machinations, has gone backwards rather than forward in the matter of domesticating wild animals.

In using the adjective *wild* it has of course to be taken into account that in different countries, in different periods in history, animals now looked upon as totally wild were in fact as domesticated, almost, as the dog. Among these, as we shall presently see, was the lion.

Even so, practically without exception our domestic animals today are those that have been domesticated since before recorded history. As P. Chalmers Mitchell, a former Superintendent of the London Zoo, wrote: "I doubt if any mammal has been domesticated in the full sense within historical times."

It is not that Man lost the notion of domesticating new species. Indeed, through the centuries it has been an ever-present thought. So recently as—speaking widely—our own times, it may not be generally known that in the earliest prospectus for the London Zoo (more properly, the Zoological Society of London), dated 1825, it is specifically proposed that "the immediate object of [this Society] will be the collection of such living subjects as may be introduced and domesticated with advantage in this country... The different races of animals employed in social life, for labour, clothing, food etc. are the direct object of its attentions... The great objects should be, the introduction of new varieties, breeds and races of animals for the purpose of domestication or for stocking out farm-yards, woods, pleasure-grounds, and wastes...

"When it is considered how few amongst the immense variety of animated beings have been hitherto applied to the uses of Man, and that most of those which have been domesticated or subdued belong to the early periods of society, and to the efforts of savage or uncultivated nations, it is impossible not to hope for many new, brilliant and useful results in the same field, by the application of wealth, ingenuity, and varied resources of a civilized people..."

Today the London Zoo is among the finest in the world: yet

even its most enthusiastic admirers will own that, except perhaps for stocking pleasure-grounds, it has as lamentably failed in these early ambitions as in its declaration from the same prospectus that "Zoology... must be regarded... as a most important branch of Natural Theology, teaching by the design and wonderful results of organization the wisdom and power of the Creator."

To some souls it will indeed teach this, but not by intention: only by the marvel of the beasts themselves.

This was no new idea. All the early naturalists saw the study of the animal kingdom as being unequivocally related to the study of the glory of God. In the Middle Ages any book on this subject was, as a matter of course, introduced by a reference to God, with the implication (or stronger) that moral benefit was to be obtained by studying the works of His hands.

Quite the reverse of this attitude, however, is reflected in the early 17th century by the Dutch theologian, Cornelius Jansen. He thoroughly disapproved. Roundly he condemns "research into the secrets of nature as a curiosity useless, indiscreet, a concupisence of the spirit". Further: "This vain love of the sciences which seduces us all the more because it has an air of honesty, but which in effect is only the culpable affectation to please his intelligence while passing by the eternal truths."

Today when we have made Science our god, it cannot but do us good to ponder on, even if we do not accept, Jansen's view.

Nearly seventy-five years after the first prospectus of the London Zoo was written, a former Superintendent, discussing the domestication of new species, wrote:

"Up to the present time these attempts have ended in failure. Without further argument, let us suppose that we obtain the young of any wild species which are easily reared by hand, and become perfectly tame as pets, we find they invariably are liable, if of a timid nature, to become alarmed and wild; on the other hand, if of a savage nature, they become dangerous and unmanageable. It appears impossible to so overcome their natural habits as to introduce them as associates of man with domestic animals. This is particularly noticeable in all the deer and antelope species, and other vegetable feeders. It is still more unlikely to succeed with flesh-eating animals." *

* *Wild Animals in Captivity* by A. D. Bartlett. 1899.

Earlier, Frederic Cuvier (brother of the famous Cuvier), Director of the Paris Museum of Natural History, who made a study of animal intelligence, had come to the conclusion that only sociable animals could be domesticated; and those who do not live in societies could be tamed, but not domesticated.

The great naturalist, Buffon, who, in the mid 18th century, had his own private menagerie for the study of animals in all their aspects, admitted a failure which will be very surprising to all who have read Gavin Maxwell's *Ring of Bright Water:* he could not succeed in taming otters!

Another Frenchman, living nearly a hundred years after Buffon, a far less erudite man, nevertheless had strong and interesting indeas on what should be the purpose of menageries. This man, Martin, was a celebrated trainer of animals for circuses and theatrical performances; and his was purely a wandering menagerie, as was common at that time.

His ambition—and it got a great deal further than a dream in his head—was to found a permanent zoo which was to be, in effect, a vast studio. Here artists and sculptors would come for their living models. As well as this, he intended encouraging farmers to study the exhibits and choose new and suitable species for working on the land; and, presumably, with an eye to novel joints of meat.

The Duchess of Berry had agreed to become Martin's patron, and he had decided to call his exhibition *Zoorama.* Unfortunately for him—and perhaps for many artists too—the Revolution of 1830 put an end to all his plans.

It is certainly matter for astonishment that no new species have been truly domesticated through so many thousands of years.

Even reindeer have not succeeded outside their native lands. In the middle of last century an effort was made to establish them in the Black Forest and near Dantzig. Neither herd flourished.

The most recent effort in this line is the current attempt to domesticate the musk-ox, a native of the bleak and bitter-cold land of east Greenland. Now, for the sake of his wool, this animal is being experimentally farmed in Alaska and in Norway.

Of course there are the silver fox, mink and other animals

farmed solely for their fur, but these are not, and have never become, strictly domestic animals.

Nonetheless, Man through the ages has consorted in no small degree with wild beasts. He is fascinated by them, and cannot, for weal or woe, leave them alone.

Our record with them—though it has its moments of beauty and its touching friendships—is indeed a deplorable one. If the Finnish legend be true, and at last the animals speak in judgement, it is like, but for the mercy of God, to go hard with us...

Doing research for this book, I have had consciously to stifle pity, or much I read would have been unbearable. But I have dwelt as little as necessary on torture, suffering and cruelty. These cannot be avoided, obviously. Yet there is the happier side. Man and the animals have an affinity that can never be lost: this, to me, is one of the loveliest and most mysterious aspects of life.

This road we have trod with the beasts is a long road, a bloody road, and the end of vileness is not yet in sight. For all that, it is a road lit always by the few in every generation who have loved, marvelled, cared, and made true friendships with the beasts. And the birds too, as we shall see later when we consider the man who could whistle swallows out of the sky to his hand.

Make no mistake: the animal kingdom is a tremendous mystery. For all the naturalists' strivings, how little we really know about this teeming life that shares our earth. What goes on in the minds of the higher animals we can try to guess, but we do not *know*. It may well be proved at last that their consciousness is far more aware than anyone has ever supposed. Who, but a score of years ago, would have imagined that a dolphin might be taught to communicate in speech with us? Maybe they knew it in the days of Alexander the Great or in the days of Augustus Caesar, when (as it is told) boys rode dolphins in the waters; and we have forgotten it since.

There is no beginning to this history I have undertaken, so we must join the road where best we can, and get glimpses here and there in many periods and in many countries of our long, long association with the feral beasts.

CHAPTER II

The First Zoo?

When one considers how greatly we ourselves marvel or gape at the splendour, the beauty, sometimes indeed at the sheer incredibility of many of the beasts standing captive in their compounds or their cages, it remains no wonder that when primitive man first saw these creatures (whatever they may have been) he tended, understandably awestruck, to see them as gods in disguise.

Many varieties of animals, from the very earliest known times, have been worshipped. Others were chosen to be totems, or emblems, of the race or tribe. In that case the animal, or bird, became sacred, since it was believed that it protected the tribe. There was often too the uneasy knowledge that the souls of the tribal ancestors were reincarnated in these alien shapes.

In this vast field we will skip the unrecorded centuries and choose as our starting place Egypt some four or five thousand years before Christ was born. This is the Egypt, give or take a few centuries, in which Moses reasoned and argued with Pharaoh and, after ten plagues, delivered from their bondage the children of Israel.

The earliest animals sacred to the Egyptians were the bull and—because it makes a perfect circle—the serpent. Some others were the baboon, the cat, crocodile, deer, even the shrew-mouse; and among birds, the ibis. When these sacred creatures died, their bodies were mummified. Thousands have been found, the bodies often in elaborate sarcophagi of granite or basalt. At Thebes were unearthed beautiful tiny coffins, some of bronze, some of sycamore, the lids finely sculpted or carved with figures of the little shrewmice whose bodies lay inside: a humble creature indeed, to our minds, to choose as divine. As recently as

1969, among many other magnificent finds, a gallery full of the tombs of sacred baboons was dug out at Saqqara. By each niche in which the mummified remains lay, or had lain, was inscribed the name of the animal, its sex, the dates of its birth and death, and here and there even its pet-name.

Not only did these sacred animals have funerals as though they were persons, but a stated period of mourning was decreed. And woe betide anyone who had been the cause of the death, even though accidentally: he too must die.

These god-creatures were kept in ornate temples, screened from common gaze by curtains woven with gold. Some had the refinement of purple carpets on which to lie. All wore ornaments. We are told of crocodiles with golden bracelets, or collars; and many of these knobbly, ungainly amphibians—who possess to so uncanny a degree the art of appearing lifeless—would come at call for their food.

And what food the sacred creatures had! Everything was of the best. Their cakes were made with honey; were they a species to fancy bird-flesh they were served with live ones caught in nets; the bulls and other vegetarian animals were given the most succulent herbage or grain to be found in Egypt.

Every aspect of their lives was thoughtfully catered for. Not only were they given warm baths and afterwards anointed with valuable oils, while perfumes burnt before them; but at the appropriate time the most perfect females of their species were presented.

There was a hard side, though, to this sybaritic life. While most of the animals appear to have had a reasonable amount of freedom, others, as has been proved by mummified skeletons, were kept so confined that their feet grew long and deformed, and in the worst cases the joints ossified.

Only people of high birth were permitted to look after the divinities; and of course sacrifices were made before them to the gods that they represented. There were ceremonies, for instance, when, before the public, a sacred crocodile devoured living prey. Then it was believed that a sick child could be healed if the invalid's head was shaved, and gold and silver of the weight of the hair was given to the crocodile's keepers. They did not, as might be supposed, keep this booty, but used it to buy food for their charge.

A little animal, greatly valued in Egypt though not sacred, was the ichneumon: a name that carries such a stigma from a repellent species of parasitic fly that it is best to use its less scientific name of Pharaoh's rat. It is a near relation of the mongoose; and the reason it was so popular with the Egyptians was because its favourite food was crocodile eggs. For, though certain crocodiles were undeniably sacred, there were rather too many of these creatures lurking by the riverbanks for the ordinary man going down to fetch his water. It used to be believed that when the crocodile was lying in his common fashion with his mouth wide open, and a certain little bird was picking the remains of meat from between his teeth, the Pharaoh's rat would take advantage of the crocodile's situation to run down his throat, gnaw his bowels, and finally eat his way out through the belly. The crocodile naturally did not survive such treatment.

This small member of the weasel family ran about the houses as domesticated as a cat today; and was certainly still doing so in Alexandria as late as the 15th century.

Another, very different animal, more or less domesticated in ancient Egypt and remaining domesticated in many countries for centuries, was the cheetah. Indeed, it is only in the last bare couple of hundred years that this animal has lost favour as one of the best hunters in the world. Those in Egypt wore collars, and were treated much like the dogs also used for hunting.

The earliest pet lion on record is probably that of Rameses II, around 1200 B.C. We even know his name. He was called Antam-nekht, and lived chained in front of the Pharaoh's pavilion.

The lion, as I have already remarked, was once a domestic animal. And if this sounds an exaggerated statement, I can only say that, in doing research for this book, nothing surprised me or impressed me more than the commonness, one might almost say the universality, of pet lions. All through the centuries, in almost every country, we find the lion, as well as being used (far, far too constantly) for contests, in the position of a free-wandering domestic animal. In old Egypt, in Imperial Rome, through the Renaissance and, occasionally, right up to recent times, the lion, and sometimes the leopard and the cheetah, are there: ornamental guards and pets of enormous social value. Status symbols, as we would say today.

But Rameses' Antam-nekht was not merely a pet. He accompanied his master in war, pacing level with the horses of the Pharaoh's battle-chariot, striking out with his claws at all who came within his distance.

Though lions were now in fashion, not everybody was allowed to keep one. It was a privilege accorded only to the wealthy. This regulation was not likely to have been made out of any consideration for the lion by ensuring that he would get sufficient to eat: simply, so noble a beast must belong only to nobles. This was usual over centuries. At one time in ancient Rome only Caesar himself might own a lion; and in other civilizations no one beneath a certain rank was permitted to keep this pet.

Besides Rameses' lion, we are told of another who, just as a dog would today, went everywhere with his master, led only by a light thong. He was taken even into temples; and was very docile, returning the caresses of all who petted him.

These lions were clipped out very much like modern show-ring poodles. The mane of course was left, with bands of fur above the paws and circular tufts on each shoulder and flank. The same mode was adopted later in Rome, with the further refinement that the manes of Caesar's lions were sprinkled with gold powder.

Here in Egypt lions, like many breeds of dogs now and in the past, were actively useful as well as being guards and companions. Not only did they go to war, but they were broken to harness and, usually a pair, put to pulling a chariot. And this would be, not as a sort of circus act, but in the streets of the city: perhaps rather a triumphal expedition than an everyday one.

A wild animal as a weapon of war was common. Other lands used different creatures to attack and terrify their enemies. Sometimes, as in India, it was elephants. (The last elephants of war surrendered to the French at Hanoi as late as 1882.) Elsewhere it might be bulls or wild boars. One can well imagine that in the days before gunpowder any such ferocious beasts would be a horribly effective weapon. Indeed, wild boars had to be given up; they were so savage that frequently they turned on the men in charge of them.

It is less easy to think of the horse as a strange and terrifying beast. Of course he has been domesticated time out of mind, but by no means in all parts of the earth. Those people called the Hyksos who conquered Egypt about 1680 B.C. completely demoralised their foe by the use of a new weapon: a strategy that has had great success even to the present day. In this case the new weapon was horses and chariots. One must suppose that it was the speed of the horses and the thunder of their feet, as well as the sight of something utterly strange, that so wrought upon the Egyptians that they scattered in confusion.

The same tactics were utterly successful over thirty centuries later when Cortes with a handful of cavalry routed the amazed and terror-struck Mexicans.

The notion of centaurs must have come from the fearsome sight of riders bearing down upon their enemies; or even, perhaps, through spectators staring aghast at alien men merely galloping for pleasure. For of course there was once a time when to back an animal was a thing unheard of.

It may be that it was the horses of the Hyksos that made the Egyptians realize that there were other animals than those to be found in their own country, wide though that variety was. At any rate it was about this time that they began to bring in animals from other parts of the world.

This brings us to the fascinating question: When and where was the first zoo* founded? So far as one can be certain of anything in these far reaches of history, it is certain that it was either in China or Egypt. China is usually given the palm. That she imported unindigenous animals earlier is proved by the ancient Chinese hieroglyphics of wild animals such as leopards, rhinoceroses and elephants.

In the province of Honan, midway between Peking and Nanking, the Emperor Wen-wang built was called the Park of Intelligence. It must have been a magnificent place, extending as it did over 900 acres, though what the inmates were we unfortunately have no very good idea: many deer, white birds "splendidly feathered", and innumerable fish. It is interesting to find this Park described as a "divine work", thus carrying out long, long before the bestiaries, the ancient notion (to which I have already referred) that the animal creation is a mani-

---

* It must of course be kept in mind that zoo is a very modern word for a collection of animals, and has not been in use very much longer than a hundred years.

festation of the glory of God, or of the gods; or indeed, perhaps in this case, of the Emperor himself.

Though the encyclopaedias give this as the first known zoo, Queen Hatasou of Egypt would appear to have been ahead by about two centuries with her collection gathered 3,400 years ago. She was the sister-wife of Thothmes III, and evidently a woman of initiative and energy.

She fitted out five ships for an expedition to East Africa (Somaliland), the intention of this armada being primarily to fetch treasures for the temple of Ammon-Ra, at Thebes. As well as the ebony, ivory, gold and myrrh for this purpose, the ships brought back many animals and birds unknown in Egypt. These included a giraffe, leopards, hares, a species of monkey and a new kind of bull. As well, these enterprising sailors carried home strange plants and even trees.

These trees (for those who are botanically minded: *Boswellia thurifera*) were shipped with the earth intact about their roots, and on arrival planted in a park near the palace.

It was in this park, now named the Garden of Ammon and placed under the protection of the sun-god, that the new animals were kept. Whether loose or in cages we are not told; but there must have been some kind of confinement, or the leopards would have preyed on the smaller creatures, if not on the valuable and fantastic giraffe.

Thothmes III was caught by his wife's enthusiasm, and he sent to Syria for more mammals, birds and plants. He himself went to the land between the rivers Euphrates and Tigris looking for elephants, and returned with the first of these beasts ever to be owned in Egypt.

However, a thousand years were to pass—and the time scale makes one dizzy—before the African species of elephant was to be tamed and trained. As everyone knows, it is the Indian elephant who is the ordinary domestic worker: Africans have never been so docile.

Later Pharaohs brought in more animals, and then the glory of Egypt began to wane. The Persians overran the country, and finally, about three centuries B. C. Alexander the Great conquered Egypt.

Under the Ptolomies the Egyptians' love of a great show of beasts flourished exceedingly. This was chiefly due to the worshipping of Dionysus (Bacchus) because, in the processions in honour of this god, it was thought proper to have as many animals as possible. A description of one of these Spring revels defeats the imagination by the sheer numbers involved. Let us look. We will leave aside most of the innumerable human beings also taking part, and attend only to the animals.

One such festival was headed by eighty-four chariots pulled by elephants. Then came sixty chariots drawn by he-goats—and small they must have looked after the elephants. But we have scarcely begun. Now there are twelve chariots drawn by lions, followed by fifteen with buffaloes in the traces, then a mere four pulled by wild asses. Stranger draught creatures come after them: of all things, ostriches; eight chariots of these; then seven pulled by stags, more by camels, down to humble mules.

This formidable procession of chariots was followed by hunters leading no less than 2,400 dogs. (Some of these would have been of the breed that we now call basenjis; for at least one fine statue of a dog found in the tomb of Tutankhamen is without any doubt at all a direct ancestor of the little African hunting-dog that has remained so pure and primitive a type to the present day.)

After the hunters came a strange and fascinating sight. Men carried trees, and to the branches were fastened wild animals and birds. One supposes monkeys, squirrels and other arboreal creatures.

It is too much to detail, too much to take in. Numbers of wild beasts followed, including a giraffe, a rhinoceros and a "great white bear", It is not believed that this was a polar bear. Most probably it was an albino; but there is a possibility that in those far times there was a genuine breed of white bear living in countries close to Egypt. Centuries later the traveller Rüppel claimed to have discovered such a species in the mountains of Lebanon.

Domestic cattle were not left out. We read with astonishment that, following a collection of animals sufficient to fill several Noah's Arks, there came two thousand bulls all of the same colour (the shade is not specified), wearing bands of gold about their foreheads, gold collars and gold shields on their chests.

How many hours did this procession, staggering in its exuberance, take to pass? It must have taken the whole day through; and finally, the climax (when the spectators one would suppose were dropping from exhaustion) came with a last chariot drawn by elephants, and on this chariot a statue in gold of the great Alexander himself.

If ever a man has deserved to have his statue cast in pure gold, perhaps it is Alexander. Less for his conquests, remarkable indeed though these were for a man who lived hardly longer than thirty-three years, than that he was the first to see in a collection of animals something having a far greater intrinsic interest than mere ornament and prestige, or (commoner still) use as a quarry for hunting. Crowding though Alexander's interests must have been, he became fascinated by natural history. Incidentally, it is claimed for Alexander that he was the first man ever to mount an elephant. However that may be, he wanted knowledge of animals, and to this end he put his old tutor, Aristotle, in charge of tremendous research expeditions, involving sending thousands of men throughout Asia and Africa. As a consequence, Aristotle, under his patronage, became the first known natural historian.

Some may prefer to give King Solomon this distinction. We know from the Bible that "he spake... of beasts and of fowl, and of creeping things and of fishes. And there came of all people to hear the wisdom of Solomon, from all kings of the earth, which had heard of his wisdom". But we have no evidence of the great king's written works on this subject, as we have the evidence of Aristotle's *Historia Animalium*.

We have been looking particularly—though very briefly—at Egypt, and there were many places in the ancient world as interesting and enthralling. But if we were to wander everywhere we would never come to an end.

Men in all countries in these unimaginably distant days of thousands of years before our own era had god-animals. Almost every creature somewhere had its devotees. The Babylonians worshipped the lion, the bull, the fish, the dove and the tortoise. In 353 B. C. they had a divine tortoise believed to be one thousand years old, and of great size. Giant tortoises do live into three figures, but a millenium sounds improbable. Like the Pharaohs, the Kings of Babylon kept many wild animals, among them rhinoceroses and elephants.

Everywhere, as the centuries progressed, there were to be found great parks full of animals that were kept solely for the chase. The beasts used for hunting them, lions, cheetahs, panthers (as well as dogs) roamed freely and unchained about the palaces. Other kings, more aesthetic, did keep parks of wild animals purely for the pleasure of looking at the creatures; but they were greatly in the minority.

Now it is time to come forward a little to the quite horrible Romans in the days of their greatness—or, I would rather say, their decadence.

CHAPTER III

The Horrible Romans

1

Anyone connecting the two subjects of early Roman history and wild animals will immediately think of the great so-called games in the amphitheatres when men fought with beasts, and beasts fought with each other. They could scarcely fail to do so. But I intend to say little of these ghastly entertainments; for a great deal has been written about them.

It was not only in Rome that it was considered a splendid amusement to put all sorts of animals together into an enclosure and watch them attack each other. These truly terrible exhibitions were to continue in appalling numbers, and in many lands, for hundreds of years. Indeed, it may be doubted if they are entirely extinct yet.

It is impossible to say when such contests began. Very, very long ago. Quite certainly bull-baiting, bear-baiting and bull-fights, whether between bulls or between men and bulls, were practised in the 2nd century B. C.

Unlucky bull! Of all the animals he in his long and bloody history has been the most consistently tormented. It goes on still ... Indeed, we should be very chary of condemning the pitiless brutality of our forefathers. Our own hands are not clean. We may have many laws now protecting animals; for all that, modern man, in the high cold names of Science and Medical Research submits creatures to, certainly very different cruelties, but nonetheless cruelties beside which many early and medieval torments pale ...

The oldest amphitheatre for animal contests was opened in Pompeii around 70 B. C. Julius Caesar founded the first in Rome.

The lust of the Romans for these spectacles and the amount of blood shed is almost unbelievable; and the wretched animals kept for the sports were ill-housed and often sick, so that they had no recompenses at all.

Not all Romans approved. Among those who would have stopped the games if he could was Seneca (born about the same time as Our Lord). But more than five centuries were to pass before Rome saw her last spectacle of warring beasts and men.* Over this period the games gradually diminished. This was partly due to so simple a reason as a shortage of animals, so heavy and for so long a time had been the slaughter. The influence of Christianity, too, played its part.

How the Romans were first stirred to the blood-lust that led to the amphitheatres is interesting, though horrifying.

It was in the year 273 B.C. that the first elephants captured in battle were brought into Rome. It is difficult for us, raised from infancy on pictures of wild animals, to imagine with what awe and baffled amazement the first elephant—or any of the more spectacular beasts—must have been seen by the common man. Quite as strange to him as though astronauts were to bring back a living creature from the moon! Of course the soldiers must have told tales of these beasts as high as a house and with a tail at either end, and carrying on their backs castles (as they did in battle) filled with soldiers. But the imagination would not take in the reality.

A few years later a Consul brought back from the war in Carthage, especially for his triumphal procession, one hundred and forty-two elephants.

This made a magnificent show, and no doubt the crowds were as impressed as the hero of the occasion desired. But then the problem arose: what to do with the great beasts afterwards? One hundred and forty-two elephants take a deal of feeding; and they were, from the Romans' point of view, useless. For more than a hundred years were to pass before the first harnessed elephants were seen in Rome, when Pompey the Great drove them in his victory procession after conquering Africa.

So the Senate decided that the herd of elephants must be killed. If they were to be killed swiftly and instantly, this would still have remained a sad and terrible decision. The reality was

* The Byzantines, on the other hand, kept up the same sort of games until the beginning of the 12th century.

horrible beyond words. They were slaughtered slowly, only by arrows and javelins, before the bloodlusting and cheering mob.

After that, and long before the organized amphitheatre games the Roman citizens demanded this "sport".

So it began. Every great general brought back wild animals of all sorts, and had them killed before the people until it became a recognized thing that this must be done. The practice did not stop with generals, either. Soon it was a matter of convention that any rich man receiving an honour, or even merely wishing to celebrate a wedding or a funeral in his family, must give a "spectacle" to the people; or, at the very least, to his guests. Thus it came about that wealthy men nearly all kept private menageries, so that they had stocks of animals on which to draw.

We may remember in passing that even here, at this period in Rome where all would seem darkness, there are shafts of light so brilliant that the many intervening centuries have not extinguished them. Everyone knows the story of the slave Androcles, who was recognized in the arena by a lion from whose foot he had once taken a thorn. If anyone is inclined to dismiss this as legend, there are other cases recorded where lions knew the gladiators, and would no more harm them than the men's own dogs.

Then there was the occasion when Pompey had decreed that a score of elephants should be speared to death as part of the celebrations at the dedication of a new temple to Venus Victrix. Darts and javelins were thrown at these poor beasts, not only by those conducting the ceremonies, but by the watching crowd too. One elephant, though so wounded that he was down on his knees, managed to get away among the people, and with his trunk to tear from their hands the weapons of any that he could reach. His comrades (Pliny tells us) "being past all hope of escaping, seemed to make moan to the multitude, craving mercy and pity with grievous plaints and lamentations; so much so that the people's hearts turned again at this piteous sight, and with tears in their eyes for very compassion they all rose up from beholding this pageant, without regard of the person of Pompey... without respect of his magnificence and stately show by which he thought to have won great applause and honour at their hands, but instead of that, fell to cursing him and wishing all those plagues and misfortunes to light upon his head, which soon after ensued accordingly."

The elephant could be an instrument of punishment too. After the Romans had defeated Persia in 168 B. C. such deserters from the army who were caught and were not of Roman citizenry, were put to death by the novel and unpleasant means of being trampled upon by elephants.

Some twenty years later, after the destruction of Carthage, Scipio Aemilianus had his deserters torn to pieces by wild animals. He made a fête of this.

Earlier, Hannibal got rid of his Roman prisoners by the diabolical device of making these late comrades-in-arms fight each other to the death. The sole survivor was then told that he must fight an elephant single-handed, and if he could win this final contest he would be set free and sent back to Rome.

Presumably his weapon was a spear, for he succeeded in killing the elephant "to the great heart's grief of the Carthaginians."

Hannibal began by keeping his word. But he thought better of it, and for what seems a scarcely adequate reason. He argued to himself that when it was learned that one man alone had killed an elephant, these beasts "would be less regarded and their service in the wars not esteemed." He therefore sent horsemen to pursue the unfortunate Roman, with orders to cut his throat. So much for Carthaginian promises!

Pliny at least doubted the value of the elephant for use in war. "These terrible beasts," (he says) "... are frightened by the least grunting of a hog, and if they are wounded at any time or put into a fight they always fall back and do as much mischief to their own side that way as to their enemies."

During the era of the amphitheatre the Romans, with few individual exceptions, saw wild animals—*all* wild animals of any size—only as something to be killed or fought against; and the numbers that they put into the arena at the same time are staggering. For one of Pompey's festivals there were six hundred lions and lionesses with twenty elephants, a lynx, a rhinoceros and, for good measure, African monkeys.

This was the very first rhinoceros to be seen in Rome; and yet Pompey could think of nothing better to do with the rare fantastic animal than put it into the arena to be killed at last.

The first giraffe, nearly a hundred years later, did not fare much better. Claudius sacrificed it, in company with four hundred lions, at the consecration of his forum. Later, giraffes (known as cameleopards) were to be very popular in the spectacles, and they were given the rather surprising nickname of "savage sheep".

When animals were killed in such quantities and over centuries, they naturally became more difficult to get, and had to be brought from further away.

Very long ago the lion was a native of Europe, but he was exterminated from his last outpost in Greece about the 3rd century B. C. So the bloodthirsty Romans, for a wonder, cannot reasonably be blamed for *that*. He was pitilessly hunted by everyone. Alas! we are only now, two thousand years later, beginning to spell out the lesson of conservation.

Every Roman who had a post abroad—and in that great Empire there were very many—was sure to be commissioned by his friends to send home any suitable beasts indigenous to that land. The Governors of colonies were even ordered by Caesar to do this. Thus thousands of animals and birds were sent from all over the world to Rome. Some came by sea, others by land; and it will surprise no one that many died on the way. The keepers, as was to happen for centuries, made money for themselves by charging for the beasts to be seen, wherever they stopped in their long slow journey.

Where there is great demand business will inevitably follow. Soon traders brought in animals too; and animals of all sorts were for sale in Rome.

All these luckless creatures—and those that died on their way were the most fortunate—torn from their jungles, their forests, were for the most part kept in close captivity: some in cages, a great number simply chained up like watchdogs. Indeed, so numerous were these beasts tied up for passing customers that there had to be a new law ensuring that the more ferocious kinds such as lions, panthers, wolves and bears were secured by sufficiently strong chains.

As well, there were parks where harmless animals roamed freely: antelope, wild asses, ostriches. All these learned to come for fodder at the sound of a trumpet. There was a special enclosure for elephants newly arrived from Africa; this was situated south of Rome, not far from the coast. At Tivoli there was a kind of hospital for sick elephants.

All sick animals had special keepers: a rudimentary veterinary service, in fact. There were two other classes of keeper: those who looked after the ordinary animals; and those who tended the ones being trained either for the games or the circuses.

Menageries were the thing. Every Caesar had one. These of course were private, and to be viewed only as a favour. However, in the ordinary way, there was seldom objection to the populace going in. These collections were a sight the visitor to Rome would be sure not to miss.

Besides, there were, at least from the century A. D., purely public menageries, known as *vivaria*.

It must be noted in passing that the word *menagerie* was originally applied only to the management of human beings: in this sense it still lingers in the word *ménage*. Only later did it come to mean, at first, the care of domestic animals. Not until the late 17th century did it acquire its modern meaning as applicable solely to a show of wild animals.

Trajan is perhaps the best-known among the Emperors as the largest animal-owner, with his collection rated at eleven thousand. Obviously it would be tedious to enumerate all the Emperors and their zoos; so we will pick points of interest here and there.

Octavius Augustus, who was born before Christ and died after His birth, had the distinction of bringing the first hippopotamus to Rome, and for this a special pond was dug. Let us hope it was allowed to live there, and was not baited to death. (Certainly many future hippopotami were.) Octavius was an enthusiastic naturalist, and all prominent Romans going abroad were ordered to report to him any curiosities they came across.

Caligula, it may be mentioned, used criminals as a supplement to the diet of his wild beasts.

It is refreshing to learn, among all the carnage that went on, that there *were* Emperors who appear to have had real affection for certain of their animals. Caracalla, for instance, had a pet lion called Acinaces (Scimitar) who sat beside him at table, and slept in his bedroom. To make more perfect the similarity to a doting owner of a lap-dog, Caracalla was often publicly seen kissing his lion!

Valentine I had two pet bears with the charming names (translated) of Innocence and Golden Spangle, and these used to sleep outside his bedroom door. A pretty effective guard, one would guess...

Heliogabalus, who, after a short interval succeeded his cousin Caracalla, was a curious character, capable on the one hand of spoiling his animals, and on the other of allowing them to be horribly cruelly handled. Among the more conventional menagerie animals he is reputed to have had ten thousand rats, one thousand mice, the same number of weasels, and a collection of scorpions.

So far as food went, his animals had the best. The dogs were fed on goose liver—a luxury then as today; while a diet of parrots and pheasants was considered suitable for his lions. Instead of going round his stables with sugar and carrots in the modern way, he handed out raisins to his horses. But he was not content with only horses to draw his chariots. He drove four-in-hands of lions, of tigers, of stags.

If the latter (with childish memories of Santa Claus) seem a not unsuitable draught animal compared with great cats, it must be stated that they are said to be the most difficult of all animals to break to harness. As for using them for riding, the only record I have found of this comes from Marco Polo. On the plains of Bargu (near Lake Baikal, in Mongolia), he says, "the most plentiful animals are stags, and I assure you they ride upon them."

According to Pliny the first person in Rome to use lions in harness was Mark Antony. He appeared in public in a lion-drawn chariot with the courtesan, Cytheris, "a common actress in interludes upon the stage... To see such a sight was a monstrous spectacle that passed all the calamities of those times." The shockingness of this sight lay far less in a great man showing himself in company with a loose woman than in the debasement of the lions. The good Romans believed then that to see such noble animals made submissive meant that "generous spirits" were about to be humbled.

Incidentally, Pliny also tells us—ignoring, or perhaps not knowing about the pet lions of ancient Egypt—that the great

Carthaginian navigator, Hanno (c. 450 B. C.), was supposed to be the first man "who dared handle a lion with his bare hand and make him follow all over the city in a slip like a dog." Hanno's fellow-countrymen were impressed, but hardly in the way he intended or expected. They decided that it was dangerous to put the liberty of the State into the hands of a man who could tame so savage a beast. So "they condemned and banished him".

Heliogabalus, whom we last left driving stags, had a very perverted sense of humour.

It was common practice at this time that fierce carnivores trained to do tricks had their teeth pulled out and their claws drawn; but it was not the custom to do this with the Emperor's own pet lions. Nonetheless, Heliogabalus secretly and vilely had it done to some of his. Why? Because it was his special amusement at a banquet, when his guests were beginning to be convivial, to let such deprived creatures loose. The unfortunate guests, not knowing that the wretched beasts were harmless, scattered in terrror and confusion. Their host found this excruciatingly funny.

Another little joke along the same lines was to let these animals into the bedrooms of his sleeping guests; thus a fuddled man would awake to the greatest alarm at seeing a bear, or maybe a lion, prowling at his bedside.

Heliogabalus also delighted in another unpleasant trick. He would send to some official what was supposed to be certain provisions for a year. When the recipient opened his vases he found, not the grain or raisins he had expected, but frogs, scorpions, snakes and other such repellent creatures. It must have been very difficult to be amused; but what else can one be when Caesar plays a practical joke?

The Roman circuses must have been astounding, and it is as well that this peak in the art of animal-training has never been achieved in the modern world.

There are contradictory accounts of the methods of training. Even in Rome not all methods were cruel.

In India about this time, Apollonius of Tyana, amazed at the freedom with which the lions, leopards and cheetahs used for hunting wandered freely in the gardens and through the palaces, questioned how such tameness had been achieved. The answer is interesting, pleasant and enlightening. "They must never be beaten, as that made them fierce and irritable; nor must one stroke them, nor coax too much, as then they become proud and more feline; but only treat them with a pleasant amiability, and caresses mingled with threats." In other words: stern kindness. Their keepers admitted to one inconvenience in leaving them so free: in springtime, with the call of mating, they were apt to run away.

Incidentally, both Aristotle and Pliny (the one copying the other) record that the Indians used to mate tigers to their domestic bitches, thus producing what were called dog-tigers, creatures formidable for hunting: so fierce indeed that they had to be bred to the third generation before the animals could be trained and handled. While it may be remarked that the tiger has never been so biddable to man as the lion, still this tale of early hunting habits can hardly be true. Not only is there the improbability of even the largest bitch being able to be covered by a tiger, but hybrids do not have progeny. (There *is* on record the case of a mule bearing a foal, but if this is true it would appear to be a unique exception.)

In Rome they were not so advanced in their ideas on animal training as the Indians that Apollonius found. What a writer at the beginning of this present century calls "modern methods" were used. That is: fasting the animals, making them exhausted, beating them and tying them up. On the other hand, they were certainly sometimes trained with gentleness, a whip used as seldom and as lightly as possible, and with caresses. As the Greeks did also, the Romans soothed their pupils with music: cithers, flutes, tambours.

As we have seen, the carnivores usually had their teeth and claws drawn—which certainly made the trainer's job less dangerous. Elephants had their tusks pulled out; and it is alleged, though it does not seem possible, that these were often dragged out by main force of man's muscle. It does not bear dwelling upon.

The description of what the finished products were able to do is almost beyond belief. Yet we cannot really doubt that most of what the early chroniclers, Pliny among them, described was true. Among the most spectacular events was an elephant walking on a tightrope, a man on his neck, and proceeding the whole width of the circus over the heads of the spectators. As a variation the elephant would walk up a sloping tightrope backwards, and slide down it again, of course head first. Another astounding trick was to show wild bulls standing upright on their hind legs in a fast-moving chariot. Not so clever an item in the programme, but one that must have brought "oohs!" and "aahs!" from the crowd was the sight of an eagle flying overhead with a young child in its talons. One wonders whether the circus-men lent their own babies for this performance, or were they slave-children or unwanted orphans?

2

Among the less attractive pets favoured by the Romans were snakes. These the owners carried with them everywhere, entwined round neck or arm. They even swarmed over the banqueting tables, and writhed across the bodies of the guests who, apparently, whatever they might think of lions, did not find the reptiles fearsome. These creatures bred so freely—and presumably many escaped—that they eventually became a plague. Fortunately, as the chronicler tells us, there were so many fires in Rome that great numbers of the eggs were destroyed.

In Greece snakes were used in a way that would strike horror to most modern breasts. In the places where the Asclepiads (or Greek physicians) treated their patients, snakes were put into the beds of those who had high fevers. The patient, feeling this surprising coolness upon his flesh, believed that a god had intervened. Perhaps in many cases faith then effected a cure.

The writer of Ecclesiastes tells us that there is nothing new under the sun. Certainly I was astounded to learn that what we call today battery farming was practised in the ancient world; and on wild birds as well as domestic ones. Hear Pliny on this subject.

"The people of Delos were the first to cram hens and pullets. With them began the detestable gluttony of eating hens and capons fattened and larded with their own grease. An act made eleven years before the third Punic war* expressly prohibited the serving at table more than one hen and that a runner and not-fed up and crammed fat. So it is that we have begun to keep fowls within narrow coops and cages as prisoners, creatures to whom Nature has allowed the wide air for their scope and habitation."

So far as domestic fowl were concerned the people of Delos, as cunning at evading the law as man has ever been, got round the new act—which specified hens and pullets—by fattening cocks and capons instead.

Pliny, however, was remonstrating against the practice of the Romans of his day of keeping wild birds intensively, as delicacies for the table. Thrushes were the most popular. They were caught in nets as they were migrating—a dreadful trade that goes on still in parts of Europe—and then fattened in small cages with scarcely any light and no windows. It was thought that if the little captives could see trees from their prison-house they would pine, and so not grow fat.

It was not only birds that were farmed in this manner. Dormice, too, were kept in enclosed tunnels and made plump. It must have taken a great number of these attractive little creatures to make one dish.

Apart from eating them, the Romans delighted in pet birds. (This fondness for being surrounded by tame birds we shall see going on for a very long time, and especially in France.) They kept all sorts. A good singing nightingale could cost as much as a slave-page or a harness-bearer. The Emperor Claudius gave a rare albino nightingale to Agrippina, that terrifying wife of his who is believed to have murdered two out of her three husbands. For this he paid the sum of six thousand sesterces, which may roughly be translated as £50, though £200 would probably be a truer price allowing for the devaluation of money. Agrippina evidently collected unusual birds. She had, Pliny tells us, "a blackbird or a thrush which could imitate man's speech; a thing never seen or known before."

He goes on to give us the surprising information that the young princes "have one starling and some nightingales taught to speak Greek and Latin. They will study upon their lessons

* c 147 B. C.

and meditate all day long, and from day to day come out with new words and be able to continue a long speech and discourse."

The Romans were in fact exceedingly good at teaching birds to speak, and it was one of their popular hobbies. Crows, rooks, magpies, jays were all taught, and these were consequently favourite pets. It is also claimed that, as well as the talking thrush, starling and nightingales just referred to, goldfinches and robins were taught to imitate the human voice.

Admittedly, this last strains credulity. Ornithologists who are wise in the construction of the vocal chords of birds will be best able to judge how many species the Romans did in fact succeed with.

For training, the birds were caged in some secluded place where they could hear no other sounds at all except the voice of their teacher. As Pliny remarks: "One must sit over them and repeat often what one would have them learn, yea, and please them also by giving them such food as they best love."

Swallows had a special use. They were the carrier-pigeons of the day, and were bred for this service. One man (at least) who was a racehorse owner would bring several swallows to the races, "and when his horse won the race he would take the birds and paint them with the colour which betokened victory and so . . . let them fly to his friends to carry tidings to them of the good success which he had obtained, knowing right well that every one would home to the same nest from whence they came."

Another instance. A swallow newly taken from her young was somehow smuggled out of a besieged city to the commander of the relieving army with the instructions "that by a linen thread tied to her foot instead of a letter, he (Fabius Pictor) should let them know, by so many knots tied in the said thread, on what day aid would arrive to the end that they also might be ready upon that day to sally forth."

It was Pliny's opinion that the swallow is the least amenable to training of any creature of the air, as—rather surprisingly— he contends the mouse is of the earth.

Whether or not these conclusions are correct it seems pertinent here to digress far in time to tell of the extraordinary power one man had over swallows. We have to make a great leap to the beginning of this century, to France. A certain M. Pays-Mellier had the gift of taming young swallows. He wrote, truly: "There is nothing lovelier than to see these birds in full liberty, in the month of May, flying at great heights, and always coming, at the least call, to perch on my finger."

Even when they were out of sight, still to his whistle the swallows would come. Visitors to his home were naturally amazed when he would take them for a long walk, and the swallows would follow all the way, coming whenever he gave his call to perch on his finger. As the French puts it: such a spectacle "les intriguait fortement".

M. Pays-Mellier tamed his swallows when they were nestlings, choosing always from the earliest broods. Presumably he built an enclosure round the natural nests; for all summer he kept them "in a large cage" at night, and loosed them at dawn. In October, when the swallows begin to gather together, on wires, on fences, he watched the companions of his summer walks joining their quite wild brethren; and presently, all together, they flew away "never to return".

At first he had tried to keep his swallows with him all winter through by housing them in a heated aviary; but he learned, as he says, that a captive swallow is "triste et peu interessant".

This gentleman, considered a rather churlish character, was greatly interested in all the animal kingdom and kept a private zoo at his home not far from Tours. Many will sympathize with his views when he told Loisel that here "was all his passion and his interest. It is amongst my animals that I find my only pleasures and my only enjoyments, for their story is more fascinating than man's; my animals are for me life-companions whose psychological character is usually more interesting than that of their master."

While on the subject of birds I cannot forbear telling of that King of Cyprus who thought up a most ingenious method of air-cooling. He anointed his body with a particular extraction from "a Syrian fruit" that had an irresistible attraction for birds. Drawn by it, they flew all about him, the fanning of their wings keeping him cool!

It is high time to go back to Rome, and to glance at the Capitol. It is not known for certain when the first lions were kept there, but it was at latest by 1100 A. D. One recalcitrant monk was fed to them after he had refused to honour Louis IV of Bavaria by ringing a welcoming peal from the Church; his reason being that Louis had quarrelled with the Pope.

The last lion on the Capitol was killed in 1414. He had escaped and killed a child. After that only domestic creatures lived there: goats, pigs, geese. It was not until as comparatively recently as 1872 that one of the city fathers had the notion of keeping on show at the Capitol a living specimen of the emblem of Rome: the famous she-wolf who nurtured Romulus and Remus.

CHAPTER IV

Of Bestiaries and Unicorns

There is not a great deal recorded about wild animals during the long centuries between the conquest of Britain by the Romans and the arrival of William the Conqueror. In all parts of the world they were still tormented and put to death for the entertainment of crowds, though less so than in the heyday of the Roman blood-letting.

A pleasant shaft of light falls through this darkness upon Charlemagne. He received from the Caliph of Baghdad (that famous Haroun-el-Raschid) the present of an elephant. Charlemagne owned many wild animals, including lions; but he was so delighted with his new acquisition, named Aboul-Abas, that for the rest of the elephant's life he took the animal with him on all his travels. When, after thirteen years, it died, a hunting-horn was made from one of the tusks; and this eventually was to be treasured, with other relics of Charlemagne, in the Cathedral at Aachen.

We hear of the first, almost certainly, genuine Polar bear somewhere around 1050 or 1060. It came from Greenland, already tame, and was presented to the King of Denmark. His Majesty's pleasure in this rarity can be gauged by the splendid presents he gave in return to the fortunate donor: a ship complete with cargo, a bag full of gold and silver, and a valuable ring.

This happened about the time the first bestiaries were being written.

These early natural history books, immensely popular—insofar as any books can be said to be popular before the invention of printing—give us some extraordinary and fascinating accounts of the animal kingdom. However absurd some of the conclusions that the authors came to, we should not dare to laugh at them. It is very nearly impossible for a man of this century, accustomed as he is to masses of information, both in word and in picture, hurled upon him by day and by night, to think himself back into a time when there were not even books. Or, rather, every book having to be handwritten, their distribution was only among the wealthy; others must go into the monasteries to see them.

No books. No cameras. Many of those who chose to write natural history books, and these were chiefly monks, had neither the means nor the opportunity to travel in order to see the creatures they wrote about. Even if they could have travelled, it would have taken them, at no pace greater than a horse's, years to cover the necessary countries. It could scarcely have been done in one man's lifetime. No wonder then if their pictures and their facts are distorted. Mostly they relied on the ancient authorities, Aristotle and Pliny. Obviously, since there were no books as we know them, much of what these great men wrote had been handed down by word of mouth, naturally enough getting garbled through the centuries.

It is always to be remembered that the bestiaries were, to a great extent, also moral handbooks. As cannot be stressed too often, all early writers on the natural world saw themselves as, first and foremost, writing to the glory of God.

The great time of the bestiaries was the 11th and 12th centuries. They began in the monasteries, inspired no doubt by the monkish custom of keeping an assortment of exotic animals, some of which—certainly the deer—must have helped to furnish the brethren's table.

In France at least, if not elsewhere, the monks probably copied the feudal lords in forcing their bears to work for their living. These poor animals, taught by God knows what cruelty, were trained to pull on the pulley-ropes that lifted blocks of stones for building; or they would turn a wheel to bring up water from a well. Sometimes they were blinded; certainly they were beaten, and kept chained up.

It may have been thought by the ecclesiastical superiors that so many animals distracted the monks from their proper pursuits. At all events the Archbishop of Paris made a start by forbidding the Canons of Notre Dame to keep any livestock except fishes, a form of food necessary for fast-days; and by the 14th century the monastic "zoo" had virtually disappeared.

The oddities recorded in the bestiaries range as widely as that the reindeer cuts down trees with his horns (and in the illustration they are saw-shaped) to the fact that elephants have no joints in their front legs.

A more bizarre belief concerned the lynx. We are told that after seven days its urine hardens, and thus are carbuncles made. The lynx, however, does not wish any of his substance to be "an ornament to the human race", and that is the reason why, when he has done urinating, he scratches sand over the puddle. (This, of course, is a natural act of cleanliness to be seen in any dog.)

One of the strangest conceptions of these early naturalists was about the birth of bears: a belief that lasted into comparatively modern times, and has permanently left in our language the phrase, *licking into shape*. The cubs (it was said), after a thirty-days gestation, were born mere blobs of pulp, and these the mother bear formed by constant licking into the correct shape of baby bears, legs and all.

There was reason behind such a notion. Bear-cubs are born hairless and blind, remaining in this condition for a surprisingly long time, for a month or five weeks, and during this period the she-bear does lick them a great deal.

Lion-cubs were thought to be born dead. On the third day the sire came and breathed in their faces, and so made them alive. We see here, of course, a confusion with Christianity. The lion in the bestiaries symbolizes Christ. Those of us who know our C. S. Lewis are inescapably reminded of Aslan ...

The tiger, on the other hand, was the embodiment of evil, being spotted with vices.

Panthers could give birth only once: their young were so eager to come into the world that they tore open their mother's womb. Which animal exactly was meant by the panther it is hard to determine. Panther was not, as today, another name for the leopard. Probably it was the serval, usually called the pard. Hence—according to early thought—the leopard: a cross between a lion and a pard. Many unfamiliar animals were considered to be hybrids. We all know of the giraffe's other name, the cameleopard. As late as the 17th century Sir Walter

Raleigh believed that the hyena was a cross between a dog and a cat. The authors of the bestiaries had a very low opinion of this animal. It could change its sex at will, "hence it is a dirty brute".

A very persistent belief concerned the eagle. It began before the bestiaries were written and had not died out in the late 18th century. Let us read a description of the "Eagle of the Sun", written *circa* 1770:

This eagle is "able to look steadfastly at the sun, even in its most refulgent splendour... They are said, as soon as they hatch, to turn the heads of their young to the eastern sun; and, if they cannot bear the light and heat, they spurn them from the nest as a spurious race."

Here again was originally a religious allegory: in looking upon the sun they were looking towards God...

One of the statements in a 12th century bestiary—vouched for by so high an authority as St. Augustine—it would be fascinating to test. It is the simple and astonishing one that the flesh of the peacock does not putrefy, or, at any rate, not for a very long time. The great Saint asks: "Who except God, the Creator of all things, endowed the flesh of the dead peacock with the power of never decaying?" There is a tradition that Augustine, when Bishop of Hippo, had experimented to find out whether this popular belief was indeed true.

It does appear to be a fact that peacock flesh, when cooked, will keep literally for years. Probably it needs the medieval cooking that included cinnamon, cloves and other spices. It used to be served as a ceremonial dish, on which a knight would make his vow before some great event, like going into battle or starting on a Crusade. The bird had been skinned before cooking, and now the skin, complete with feathers, was replaced, and the feet and bill gilded. On these occasions only sometimes was the meat eaten; more often it was a feast only for the eyes, and was kept to be used again. Aldrovandi (the 16th century naturalist) writes of a peacock killed and cooked in 1592, and six years later still being free of any bad smell. The pheasant was sometimes used for these knightly ceremonies; but for a long time the peacock was considered the particular food for knights and lovers.

The peacock is perhaps the most beautiful of all birds, certainly the showiest, and he has his vanity too. This does not extend to his feet. According to the Roman poet, Martial, the reason why peacocks make so ear-splitting, raucous a noise is, that upon catching sight of their feet, they shriek with horror because they are so little in keeping with the glory of their plumage!

In a very early account of a royal menagerie the author had probably got most of his "natural history" from a bestiary. He may well have helped to compile one. This was a French monk, Raoul Tortaire, living in the 12th century, who chanced to see the King's procession at Caen, in Normandy, and described it—writing in Latin, of course—in a letter to a friend.

His attention was first taken by a young lion, only six months old, who roared so mightily that he alarmed everyone in the crowd, as he was led along by his African keeper—and this man, with his unusual skin, must have been as interesting to the spectators as any of the beasts. The pair were followed by a horse on which was sitting a magnificent leopard. This animal, Raoul informs his correspondent, is a cross between a pard and a lioness, hence its name. A lynx interested him too, the keeper holding up its cubs. The camel, says Raoul, may live to be a hundred years old. It can go without water for four days; and on the fourth day it drinks enough to last it four days more. It is best, he adds, to castrate a male camel if it is to be used for carrying loads. His final remarks are on the ostrich. This bird can digest iron as though it were liquid food. A belief, as we shall see, not to be discarded for a very long time, and which, indeed, caused the death of many unfortunate ostriches.

Though perhaps by this time people no longer believed in centaurs, other mythical animals such as the gryphon and the unicorn featured in the bestiaries. Speculation on the origin of these and similar creatures is fascinating. Belief in them died slowly.

But of all the mythical creatures it is the unicorn who holds greatest sway over human hearts.

Is he truly fabulous?

Who that has a spark of poetry in him can utterly repudiate that "noble and unmated beast . . . Oh golden hoofs, oh cataracts of mane . . . Oh the neck wave-arched, the lovely pride . . ."?*

---

* *The Late Passenger* from Poems by C. S. Lewis.

Surely, surely, somewhere in the dim avenues of time there must have roamed this glorious great horse, central-horned, milk-white, smooth or shaggy according to our fancy, who stood and still stands for purity and mystic holiness.

It seems impossible that Man could have invented the idea of him from—as the practical people tell us—the slender evidence of a narwhal horn washed up upon some beach a thousand thousand years ago.

Rumour indeed credits Alexander the Great's famous horse, Bucephalus, as having been a unicorn. Marco Polo, writing of Badakshan, in Afghanistan, tells us uncopromisingly that "once there were in this country horses descended from the breed of Alexander's horse, Bucephalus; they were all born with a horn on their head, like their ancestor, Bucephalus. The only person to possess the breed was an uncle of the King's who refused to let the King have one, so the latter had him killed. The widow then, in despite, destroyed the whole breed, so that now it is extinct."

For all this, Marco Polo obviously did not see Bucephalus and his descendants as true unicorns. Certainly he, with other early travellers, confused the rhinoceros with the unicorn. So he described these beasts when he journeyed into Sumatra (known to him as Basman or Bassyna):

"... little less than elephants, having a head like a swine, and always hanging it downward to the ground, and standeth with a good will in a miry puddle. They have but one horn in their forehead, whereby they are called unicorns, their horn is large and black, their tongue is rough and full of prickles long and thick."

Marco Polo has the grace to add that a very different idea of the unicorn is held in Europe, and he could not imagine that this black and miry beast would ever wish to lay its head in a virgin's lap!

No, the unicorn is far other than the rhinoceros. *That* is not the animal of whom the Psalmist sings, the animal of whom the Lord, out of the whirlwind, demands of Job: "Will the unicorn be willing to serve thee, or abide by thy crib? Canst thou bind the unicorn with his band in the furrow? or will he harrow the valleys after thee? Wilt thou trust him because his strength is great? or wilt thou leave thy labour to him? Wilt thou believe him, that he will bring home thy seed, and gather it into thy barn?"

Unquestionably this creature is an equine. One could at least *dream* about putting him to the plough...

Pause, and wonder: Why has the unicorn, more than any other beast, so agelessly caught at men's imaginations that even to this day, in a clangorous, iron-cluttered world, the sound of his name fills us with a yearning for the lands of faery and all that those words promise? Superb and splendid beast! We shall long in vain for you until the end of time...

There have been clumsy human efforts to "make" unicorns. For the purposes of the amphitheatre games in Imperial Rome, the oryx, when young, had his tender horns bound together, so that, after the manner of grafting, they grew together. The idea behind this was that one straight horn was a better weapon than two. But this, of course, could not but remain a backward-pointing horn.

Very much nearer our own time experiments were made with young bulls. The horn-buds were removed, and one was implanted into the centre of the forehead. This grew, thus proving to the satisfaction of these scientific meddlers that a beast with a single frontal horn was not, as had been suggested, a biological impossibility. This is all it could prove; and the resulting creature, far from being graceful and awe-inspiring, must have looked the freak that it was, with this curved and obviously bovine horn.

If we must remain mystified as to the origins of the unicorn, those of that other popular creature of myth, the dragon, are easier to explain.

There do exist enormous lizards, such as the komodo dragon, and these, to a man affrighted, may well have seemed more monstrous than they are. But more probably the idea of the dragon—and indeed the gryphon—comes from ancient tales of hearsay, and race-memory too, of the pterodactyl or some other prehistoric flying reptile. Certainly he is known over most of the earth; and everywhere, except in China and Japan, stands for evil as the unicorn stands for virtue.

CHAPTER V

Early Days at the Tower

Although it is a tremendous step—a thousand years, no less—from the days of ancient Rome to the time when the bestiaries were being written and the little "zoo" that is the direct ancestor of the great London Zoo of today was founded, yet there is a connecting bridge.

When Julius Caesar conquered the Anglo-Saxons in 55 B. C. the invaders discovered, to their surprise, that the wealthy among these barbarians, the lords of England, kept certain creatures in enclosures. Nothing very interesting: merely hares and poultry. The point was that they kept these captives *not*—as would have seemed right and sensible—for food, but simply for their own pleasure.

This was an attitude which naturally dumbfounded the Roman soldiery. For them animals of whatever kind existed only to be useful, whether for draught or as food or to offer sport in the amphitheatres. That anyone should simply wish to look at them, play with them, or admire them for their beauty and grace, was an idea that had hitherto never occurred to them.

At least the Romans appear to have allowed the subject race to continue to indulge this whimsical and useless pursuit. At the same time we need not doubt that a hungry legionary helped himself to hare or goose as he passed through the countryside.

The English forests—and, for certain, some of the lords' enclosures—were soon to have a new animal. The fallow deer is not indigenous here: he was imported by the Romans. It was not until the 13th century that this deer spread to France, brought, in his turn, by an English nobleman.

But if the Romans left the small, humble enclosures in

peace, it was a different matter when William the Conqueror came. The Norman lords seized these reserves, now grown of course bigger and more interesting, and claimed the animals for their own. Thus they formed the first hunting forests and parks, stocking them with deer and other suitable animals. One of the oldest of these reserves is Chillingham, where the white cattle are famous to this day.

Another very ancient breed of cow, indeed claimed to be the oldest of all domestic cattle in this country, is the Old Gloucester.

William the Conqueror chose as his English residence the Manor of Woodstock; and there our early Kings continued to live. Very soon, following the universal habit of royal prestige gained by owning exotic animals, a few wild beasts were brought there; and, as we shall see, Woodstock is therefore the first, remotest ancestor of the London Zoo.

The earliest news of beasts being kept at Woodstock comes from the chronicler Lambert d'Ardre, who tells of a bear from there being given to his master (as we should say, employer) by William Rufus.

But it was Rufus's successor, Henry I, who came to the Throne in 1100, who enclosed Woodstock "with a wall, though not for deer, but for all foreign wild beasts, such as lions, leopards, camels, linxes, which he procured abroad of other Princes; amongst which, more particularly, says William of Malmesbury, he kept a porcupine... covered over with sharp-pointed quills, which they naturally shoot at the dogs which hunt them." So wrote the 17th century Dr. William Plot in his *History of Oxford*. The collection also included a rare owl, the gift of William de Montpellier.

As was the custom then, and for a long time afterwards, the King, when he journeyed about his realm, or even when he went to war, was always accompanied by some of the inmates of his menagerie.* These were an outward and visible sign of his royalty.

It may sometimes be wondered why the leopard, an animal native of a country so very far from our own, is included in the heraldic arms of England. Henry I had a particular interest

* I use the word throughout for convenience; but it must be remembered that it did not have its modern sense until the 17th century.

in animals from the East; and the leopard as a royal device dates from his reign.

As for the Lion and the Unicorn: the lion from time immemorial has been the symbol of royalty; the origin of the unicorn (from Scotland) is more obscure. But it is evident that the two together stand for Royalty and Virtue.

It was in 1235, in the reign of Henry III, that the beasts at Woodstock were moved to the Tower of London, and there a menagerie was to remain for the next six hundred years.

It was sixteen years after this move that the famous white bear arrived: almost certainly an albino and not a polar bear. He was famous for more than being a novelty to the populace. Alarmed by now at the cost of keeping so many wild animals, the King decided that his new acquisition should be at the charge of the city of London. Forthwith the Sheriffs were ordered to find the money to cover both the cost of feeding the animal and the wages of the keeper.

The Sheriffs who, understandably, did not care for this pronouncement, grudgingly allowed fourpence a day. Whether the sum was not enough, or the keeper intended the bear to feed as cheaply as possible so that his own profit would be more, whatever the reason, the bear was set to provide at least some of his sustenance by his own effort. Every day he was to be seen, on a chain and muzzled, being led to the banks of the Thames. Here his leading-chain was exchanged for a long rope, his muzzle removed, and into the water he went to catch his dinner. In those days of course the Thames was teeming with fish; and so it remained until less than two hundred years ago.

It was not long before His Majesty, delighted at the financial convenience of having his bear supported, decided that the cost of his entire menagerie housed in the Tower should be borne by the city of London. Grumble the Londoners might, but the thing was done, and this arrangement was to last for at least a hundred years.

Much worse than the bear, and a few lions and leopards, was to come. The then King of France, Louis IX, presented his brother-in-law, the King of England, with an elephant. There was no suitable accommodation in the Tower for so vast a beast; so the unfortunate city fathers were commanded to build an appropriate dwelling. Allowing for the fact that the elephant would almost certainly be led about the streets daily, they built a reasonably adequate one: it measured forty feet by twenty.

Although the Sheriffs must have been apprehensive about the cost of feeding the giant—and all this on top of the huge, strongly-built cage—everyone awaited the elephant's arrival with keen excitement and curiosity. No one had ever seen an elephant.

Their expectations were more than fulfilled.

The crowds were fascinated, enthralled. The creature was, as Ralph Holinshed, the 16th century chronicler records, "a beast most strange and wonderful to the English people, sith most seldome or never any of the kind had been seene in England before that time."

It is possible, though not certain, that an elephant had been shown in England under the Roman occupation. Still, that was a thousand years ago, and one can imagine the excitement, the pushing crowds. Or can one? This exhibit was as alien, as marvellous as something from, if not another world, another age, forgotten. It was, almost, as though the London Zoo tomorrow wast to announce that they had a brontosaurus on view...

So the years passed; and as it was the habit of prices (then as now) to rise, so in later reigns the Tower animals' allowances (still at the cost of the city of London) increased first to sixpence a head a day, and finally up to two shillings and a penny: a fair sum of money at that day's value. Edward II's lion, by his own order, was fed a quarter of a sheep each day. Keepers' wages were rising too. By Edward III's time they had come up from the original penny-halfpenny a day to sixpence. Incidentally, the very first zoo-keeper whose name we know lived in this reign. Probably he was a Frenchman: at any rate he was called Berenger Candrer. Sixpence a day was, at that period, a good wage, and made quite inexcusable the pilfering by the keepers of the money intended for the animals' food. Thus, through their guardians' selfish and cruel greed the unhappy Tower inmates became more and more sickly until, by 1436, there was not one lion left alive.

A few poor beasts of not much account remained at the Tower. Nine years passed. Then Henry VI married Margaret of Anjou, and things were changed.

This young girl—she was only sixteen—was the daughter of

René, Count of Anjou, bearing also the titles of King of the Two-Sicilies, Duke of Lorraine and Bar: a remarkable man. He was passionately interested in animals, and owned the biggest collection of wild beasts in the whole of France. His interests extended in this line beyond the animal kingdom. He also collected men of different races and, therefore, of very different appearances. Such a bizarre habit was by no means uncommon. Before travel became general and when there were few books and pictures, and these costly, it may easily be imagined that to any European a Negro (for instance) was as great an object of curiosity as though he were a species of exotic animal: indeed, since he was also a human being, a great deal more so. At all times, and in various parts of the world, along with freaks, black men, Red Indians, Esquimaux and other races were kept on show in a kind of free captivity for people to gape at or, more often, solely for the prestige and pleasure of the monarch. We shall be looking later at some of these "human zoos".

As well as these slaves—for they were no better—René's enthusiasm extended to all with unusual skills and who were in a position to choose whether or not they should come to his Court. He liked to gather about him conjurors, jugglers, tightrope-walkers, even writers of morality plays, and jesters of exceptional wit.

However, in England it was for his splended menagerie that the Count of Anjou was chiefly famous; and it must soon have been bruited about that other members of his family shared his fondness for keeping wild animals: notably his sister, the Queen-Consort of France and her son, the future Louis XI.

Thus it was that Margaret of Anjou, the royal bride, arrived here with the reputation that she too loved exotic beasts. Hence, on her landing in England she was presented with a lion.

Margaret, graciously accepting it, sent the animal to the Tower. It was no doubt through her influence that more lions were given, or sent for from abroad. Soon the decaying Tower menagerie began again to thrive. It is from this date that the post of Keeper of the Tower Lions became one of the most important Court appointments, always being given to a person of quality. We may safely presume that his actual duties were far from burdensome, but he was paid a salary of sixpence a day, as well as receiving sixpence a day for each animal under his charge: a very pleasant emolument. The first holder of this title was one Robert Mansfield.

In the following reign, that of Edward IV, the lions' accommodation was moved to another part of the Tower, and there the beasts were to be seen for the next four hundred years. The entrance to this section still bears the name of the Lion Gate. The cages or, rather, dens were built in a semi-circle, the barred arches through which the spectators looked being twelve feet high. The area in front of these dens was large enough to allow for baiting the wretched animals, or to stage fights between them. These entertainments were watched from a railinged promenade running above the arches of the dens. The famous Lion Tower, however, was not built until the reign of Elizabeth I.

It was against the law, and remained so till the 18th century, for anyone but the monarch to exhibit wild animals. The only exceptions to this royal prerogative were "Thomas Dymocke, and the Keeper of His Majesty's Lions for the time being". The Dymockes of course were privileged as the hereditary King's Challengers. Anyone else trying to make money in this way was warned in a public notice that it was the King's right, and if they offended they would "answer the contrary at their perils".

CHAPTER VI

Of Lions and Bears

The lion, whose noble, calm, supercilious mien can, even when he is caged, make one feel insignificant, is rightly dubbed the King of Beasts. If our remote ancestors did not actually call him so, they recognized the title for all that. As we have seen, the common man was not usually permitted to keep a lion.

In nearly all States he has been a symbol of royalty. This was so in ancient Egypt, in Imperial Rome before its worst days of decline, through the Renaissance, right up to modern times. Here we may mention in passing that to this day—at least at the time of writing—the Emperor Haile Selassie of Abyssinnia keeps up this old and noble practice. His lion, Tojo, to be met with as a lesser person's dog is to be met with, has rendered uneasy many visitors to the Palace!

These are all living lions. If we go back to the 10th century to Byzantium (Constantinople), we find that the Byzantines, not content with real lions, or perhaps finding them a good deal more trouble, had them sculptured life-size in gilded bronze, and with the ability both to roar and to lash their tails. The actual mechanics of these fascinating "toys" have long puzzled scholars. Not only lions were thus made lifelike. Bishop Liudprand of Cremona tells us in his *Antapodosis*: "Before the Emperor's seat stood a tree, made of bronze gilded over, the branches of which were filled with birds, also made of gilded bronze, which uttered different cries, each according to its varying species." The Emperor's throne "was of immense size and was guarded by lions, made either of bronze or of wood covered over with gold, who beat the ground with their tails and gave a dreadful roar with open mouth and quivering tongue... At my approach the lions began to roar and the birds to cry out, each according to its kind." Liudprand goes on to say that he was "neither terrified nor surprised", as he had already heard of these wonders.

Whatever his true feelings about the lions, he was certainly startled by the throne itself. It "was so marvellously fashioned that at one moment it seemed a low structure, and at another it rose high in the air". The Bishop had been brought into Constantine's presence by two eunuchs; and after he had made obeisance three times, with face upon the ground, "Behold! the man whom just before I had seen sitting on a moderately elevated seat had now changed his raiment and was sitting on the level of the ceiling ... On that occasion he did not address me personally, since even if he had wished to do so the wide distance between us would have rendered conversation unseemly."

So, from his lofty height the Emperor spoke to Liudprand through an intermediary.

Writing of another visit to Constantinole about twenty years later (in his *The Embassy to Constantinople*), Liudprand recounts that after a visit to the Palace he "was taken back to the five lions who were my fellow-citizens and housemates in the aforesaid hateful house". It has been suggested by one competent to know* that these were the same sort of mechanical lions described in Liudprand's earlier work. Yet... yet I cannot help thinking it just as likely—indeed, more likely—that five living lions did roam the Bishop's house. Right up till the 16th century lions were common in Constantinople. The Roman games had lingered here longer than anywhere else; and they did not die out for at least one hundred and fifty years after Liudprand's visit.

The instances of tame, virtually domestic lions attending Kings or their viceroys (and why not their eminent visitors?) are legion.

We find in Spain in the 15th century a "very large lion" lying at the monarch's feet when he receives foreign ambassadors.

On to the 18th century, and at Scutari the Sultan's minister has a lion playing in the palace with as much freedom "as the most peaceful and domestic animal".

At the same period it is recorded that in great houses in both

* F. A. Wright, translator of *The Works of Liudprand of Cremona* 1930, to whose book I am indebted for the above extracts.

Algiers and Tunis lions came and went at will, and were to be seen playing with the servants.

More alarming in the next century were the lions of Ahmed Bey, the last governor of the city of Constantine in Algeria. He owned several, all of which he tamed himself; and always two of his finest walked or lay beside him. At his levees they waited at his feet. When, as from time to time happened, he became angry, the pair of lions responded to their master's displeasure by standing up and growling. This, not surprisingly, terrified the petitioner who, fearful that at any moment he might be set upon, began to tremble and quake. Ahmed Bey, with perhaps a macabre sense of humour, found this so comical that his wrath turned to amusement. He would then stroke his tail-lashing lions, and pardon the offender.

A bare century ago the then King of Abyssinia, when he received English Ambassadors did so with four lions beside him. It happened that these lions presently came to Queen Victoria as trophies of war. She "hastily" gave them as a present to the King of Sardinia.

Even more recently an interesting account of lions living in quite extraordinary harmony with men is given by the traveller, V. L. Cameron, in his account of his journeyings to Africa in 1877. He describes a village on the border of Lake Tanganyika where, for twenty-five years, a band of lions had lived among the people without hurting anyone. They were venerated as totems of the tribe; and on festive days were given goats, sheep and honey. At first reading one pictures a small pride of these favoured beasts living so amiably. One is quite wrong. Mr. Cameron states that as many as two hundred could be seen; and—more amazing still—each had a name to which he (or she) would come when called. When one of these lions died, he was mourned for as though he had been a member of the family.

This, alas! is a very rare instance of man and beast in brotherhood. Mostly it is the same sad, dreary story: contests and gore, century upon century ...

Let us now look at the Florentines, who were famous in the 14th century for their lion-keeping. It was no new thing for the Florentine ruler to have lions. At the very beginning of the Christian era they were kept for the annual games held in honour of the Roman Emperors. Darkness falls here, as over most places, for the next thousand years. Probably lions were kept, if on and off, all that time. Certainly in 1293 a new lion house was built.

By the 14th century there were twenty-four lions, looked after by three keepers. Only now were the true facts of lion birth understood. It had been accepted for centuries—as we saw in the bestiaries—that the little creatures had no life until the sire had breathed it into them. It must have been very surprising, and perhaps disappointing, to find that in this respect lion cubs were no different from puppies or kittens!

The staple food of these lions was, as elsewhere, sheep. Indeed, throughout the Middle Ages and later, sheep farms were frequently adjacent to the menageries chiefly for this purpose.

In this connection it is interesting to note that in Ghent in 1420, where the King allowed the town butcher to exhibit four royal lions for his own profit, the man had to raise his entrance fee because, owing to the war between France and England, the price of sheep had risen steeply.

It is not pleasant to learn that Lorenzo the Magnificent (Medici ruler of Florence in the 15th century) fed living lambs to his lions. One suspects that this would not have been uncommon.

But far worse is the story of the sick lion at Vincennes two hundred years later. To tempt its appetite its keepers skinned the wretched lambs alive before presenting them to the invalid. Mercifully for future lambs, this diet was found not only to do no good, but to be positively harmful. The French author, Charles Perrault (he who gave us such famous fairy-tales as *The Sleeping Beauty, Red Riding Hood, Cinderella*) dissected the lion after its death, and pronounced that the skinned lambs had "engendered too much blood", for Nature intended animals of prey to devour skin, fur and feathers, these being necessary correctives to the digestive system.

After this grisly digression it is time to return to Florence.

The Florentines were superstitious about their lions. If one of them died, they knew that this foretold calamity; just as the birth of cubs was an excellent omen for the city.

It must have been only if the death of a lion was from sickness or natural causes that any ill-luck would ensue; for the lions' lives were frequently risked in combat. No doubt, however, it was anticipated that, as the more powerful beasts, the lions would most often be victorious.

Curiosity as much as lack of compassion must have inspired these ever-popular entertainments of contests between so many oddly assorted animals. Simply the question: what would *happen*? In one picture of a Florentine "sport", in the arena together are such diverse animals as a lion, three dogs, a bull and a mare.

While these amusements appear to us quite indefensible, we have to remember that it is very difficult to judge people who lived so long ago, in so different a world. Their values were not our values; and if they reckoned animal life cheap, they reckoned human life equally so. Besides, as I have already remarked, we ourselves do not stand in a strong position to condemn. With the exception, however, of one great and hopeful difference. Though always there must have been the few who were anguished by so much animal suffering, it was only as recently as the last century that laws and, what can often be more potent, public opinion came down at all on the side of the animals...

In 1459 when the Pope, Pius II, and a member of the distinguished Italian family of Sforza were to visit Florence, Cosmo of Medici, ruler of this independent state, decided to revive a spectacle in the manner of those of ancient Rome. The lion population in Florence was now twenty-six, and Cosmo had besides many other beasts. For his grandiose scheme there was no arena in the city big enough. So he decided to hold his games in the vast courtyard of his Palace. Workmen were ordered to block the ways in and out, thus forming the enormous enclosed area required.

The great day came. The distinguished guests, with retinues, settled themselves comfortably at Palace windows overlooking the courtyard. Lesser folk watched from higher and more distant windows.

With fanfares and flourishes the wild animals were let loose. These were the twenty-six lions, wild boars, wild bulls, savage horses, wolves, hunting-dogs and a few other miscellaneous creatures. Exactly the hotch-potch of diverse ferocious beasts which the Florentines loved to see. Immediate and terrible carnage was expected.

Minutes passed. The audience stared, became impatient. Whisperings, foot-tappings, uneasiness.

For nothing at all was happening.

It had not for a moment been foreseen that all the other animals, supposedly so fierce, would be so terrified of the great troop of lions that they would scatter in confusion, get out of their way, and think not at all of attack, but only of saving their own skins. In this they became allied refugees from a common enemy.

The lions, for their part, ignored every other animal in the arena. For a few minutes they prowled about the great space; and then, instead of leaping upon one of the many choices of prey as the audience a-tiptoe with expectation waited for, they quietly went and lay down, all together, in one corner, away from their terror-stricken companions.

One can imagine the general indignation; imagine too the red face of Cosmo, so humiliated in this great show he had been at such pains to prepare.

Obviously something must be done. Keepers and servants were summoned, orders given.

Presently there rolled out into the courtyard a huge grotesque wooden model of a giraffe. In this contraption (as in the Trojan horse of old) were concealed men, no less than twenty of them. They made the thing move towards the recumbent lions. Either the beasts had seen it before, or it made no horrific impression upon them. They remained lying down.

The defeated giraffe-men gave up, and rolled themselves away. By and by, after further consultations, the impatient spectators saw another "engine" coming into the arena. This was a device that the Florentines had copied from the Turks. It was an enormous wooden ball, full of slits and holes. Inside the ball crouched a man holding a sword. His vehicle was so constructed that he was able to make it roll; so it must have contained an ingenious gyroscopic platform for him to stand on. The ball rolled towards the lions who, still peaceable, would have continued to ignore it as they had ignored the giraffe. But this was a subtler instrument. The unfortunate lions found themselves being pricked by the sword through the holes in the ball. This was too much. The account says that this means "just succeeded in making them respond". We learn no more, but we can thankfully assume that what was intended to be a bloodbath was at least something a great deal less.

This type of ball was used for provoking animals right up till the 18th century.

The Florentines were fond of unusual contraptions for managing their wild beasts. Much later than Cosmo's time they had what is described as an "ingenious machine" for persuading the lions to return to their dens. It too was made of wood, and painted on it was "the shape of a terrifying monster. Two men are enclosed in it and make it move towards the lion, at the same time throwing rockets which appear to come out of its jaws, so that the lion, frightened by the fire, immediately retreats to his den, where he is easily shut up."

About this time—mid-18th century—there was a fire in the menagerie whereby many of the animals escaped and caused "divers accidents in Florence".

Not only in Florence, everywhere the contests went on. The animals might occasionally tire of the incessant battles. The humans, for century upon century, never tired at all.

In the Tower of London lions were sometimes put to maul a bear; and this was the punishment decreed for a bear which had killed a child. It was hardly undue viciousness on the part of the bear because, as is recorded, the child had been "negligently left in the beare-house". In this case the lions, as in Florence so many years earlier, would not attack the bear. Rather surprisingly, he was not immediately dispatched by some more eager carnivores; for the moment he was spared, only to be baited to death two weeks later. Then the mother of the "murthered" child was given £20 out of the takings.

Bears have not always hurt children who crept into their cages. There is a charming story about a little boy who sought shelter in a bear-pit in Lorraine. The winter of the year 1729 was bitterly cold. This homeless child, desperate for warmth, squeezed into the pit where a bear called Masco was kept. Masco, as though he knew just why his little visitor had come, took him between his great furry legs, and held him against the warmth of his chest. As soon as it was day the child ran off again to the town. At night he returned. And so he lived: a beggarboy by day, a bear's companion by night. Masco grew so fond of him that he would save some of his own food for his little guest. And if you have no regular meals, you will not despise a bear's victuals.

Nothing was known at first of this strange companionship. The boy was discovered only by the chance that one evening the keeper brought Masco's food later than usual. To his astonishment the animal did not come forward for his meal. The man looked more closely at his charge. The bear was crouched, his eyes shining; and the keeper saw, between his paws, the boy fast asleep.

This story excited the sympathy of everybody, including those at Court. It is sad to have to say that their kindly intentions of help for this waif came too late. He died soon after; and it is certain that though he had no kith nor kin to mourn him, the bear who was his warmth and comfort missed him.

The bears kept in pits were more fortunate than some: that is, if we discount the fact that any day they might be taken out to be baited. In Denmark in the 16th century bears were to be seen wandering loose in and around at least one of the royal residences; as a safety measure these brutes had their front paws tied to their backs. Such cruelty was not even always effective: one managed to bite a child in the head, and then break his ribs.

Perhaps the palm for brutal behaviour to bears can go to Russia. The Russians did dreadful things with bears. I will tell of only one of them. It is so horrible it is almost unbelievable, involving, as it does, a man as well.

This was some people's idea of a joke. A half-starved bear was tied to a ring fixed strongly in one corner of an empty room, with a chain just long enough so that the bear could nearly, but not quite, reach the diagonally opposite corner. Then an unsuspecting "friend"—one known as a "novice" who had not heard of this macabre buffoonery—was shown the bear, given a quick push inside as if by accident and the door locked on him. He seldom reached the only safe corner swiftly enough; and when, with arm or leg torn he did so, there he had to stand, tight upright against the wall, while the bear, tortured by hunger and frustration, growling and furious, tried to reach him . . .

The poor bear has the unenviable record of probably being, after the bull, the most consistently abused animal in entertainment.

Old people living today may still remember seeing in their childhood, even in England, a man with a dancing bear going from village to village. By the beginning of the present century, though, dancing bears had been outlawed in many towns throughout Europe. The owners, thus deprived of their living, were going overseas with their "canary-birds", as they called them, to America, and even Australia. Probably there are dancing bears still in the world, but no longer, mercifully, in the great centres of civilization.

It was an old practice.

No doubt many of these bears were bred in captivity. Wild cubs, when they were caught, were taken with mankind's usual treachery. While small they were fed and, seeing men as their friends, they thus became quite tame. By and by, while the cub was climbing a tree, a rope was wound round him, fastening him to the trunk so that he could not move. Then and there a ring was thrust through his tender upper lip, then a muzzle put upon him.

His tortures were by no means over. At Smorgony in Lithuania, there was a famous school for training bears. It bore the deceptively amusing title of the Bears' Academy. The luckless pupils were heavily muzzled; and had a T-shaped iron bar thrust through the hole in the upper lip, the horizontal bar of the T being covered by the flesh, and a chain attached to the protruding shaft. It needs little imagination to realize the pain of any pull on that chain. The animals were then taken to what was called the Beginners' Room, which had a floor quite considerably heated. Now, the soles of a bear's feet are very tender; and before coming into this room the pupil had his hind feet bandaged. The pain of the burning on the pads of his forefeet made the bear stand upright; and thus, with the cruelty of his snout-chain, he learned to dance—for the delight of children and simple people who did not know (and did not care) how he had come to this accomplishment.

What an irony it is that this great, awkward, stumbling, furry beast that we have so long, and till so recently, dreadfully abused, should have come to be at last, in the form of the Teddy-bear, a tremendous solace to hundreds of thousands of children!

CHAPTER VII

Of Tigers

Reading the old accounts of the hunting, the parades, the pets, one is struck by, more than anything else, the apparently casual way in which normally fierce beasts went everywhere. True, occasionally there were accidents and somebody was killed, but such an occurrence seems to have been a great exception. One asks: What power had our ancestors that we have lost? Everywhere, in every country, lions, leopards, cheetahs wander, controlled seemingly by no more than a silken leash. They lie at the feet of ladies; they are household pets.

Not so tigers, however. The tiger remained unknown in the western world all through the Middle Ages until the end of the 15th century. Marco Polo, who presumably had never knowingly seen one, misnames them in his *Travels* as lions, supposing them, one concludes, to be an unusual species of Chinese lion. They must have been tigers, for he describes them thus: "They have very fine coats and are of a beautiful colour, being striped lengthwise in black, red and white." *Lengthwise* is baffling, but by the time he came to write his *Travels*, his visual memory may well have failed him.

These beasts were evidently common in those days of the Kublai Khan in Peking or—to give the city the name it was then known by—Cambaluc. When the Khan went out on his hunting expeditions all his personal tents (they were pavilions rather than tents, as we understand the word) were covered with these skins, which we will henceforth roundly call tiger. Inside, the tents were lined with ermine and sable: furs which even then, in the 13th century, were, as Marco Polo remarks, "the most beautiful, fine and costly furs in existence". Another touch of luxury was the silken guy-ropes.

The Khan's tigers were trained to hunt; and it was almost certainly a tiger (though described as a large lion) which, at the great feasts, crouched down before the Khan, "making signs of obeisance, and you would think it knew him for its lord and master. It remains before him unchained. And truly it is a marvellous sight."

Before watching a hunting expedition of the Khan's, it will be worthwhile to see how the prey was taken from all these fierce hunting-animals: leopards and cheetahs more commonly than tigers.

One must again repeat that the early collections of wild animals—to be found in practically every country—were only very rarely assembled for pleasure. The prime motive was prestige; and the creatures were there, not to be admired, but to fight each other or to hunt with or be hunted.

Cheetahs and leopards were commonly used by the nobility for coursing from very early times right up to the 18th century and later. What seems incredible to minds accustomed to regarding the horse as a highly nervous animal was the matter-of-fact manner in which the great cats, when not actually in pursuit of prey, were carried on the backs of the horses behind the saddle. This is true beyond any doubt. There are many contemporary pictures of these hunters on the croup behind their masters. Marco Polo too expressly says that thus the great Kublai Khan went hunting. So, his work done, the leopard or cheetah was trained to leap up again to his seat on the horse's haunches. What modern horse would not go into a frenzy of terror!

A hare was a frequent quarry. As soon as the hunter sighted one, the leopard was given his orders. He chased and caught the hare, the rider keeping up with him. There must of course have been many occasions, especially with the speedy cheetah, when the rider was out-stripped and did not arrive in time to retrieve the game. But, in general, he kept up and, at the moment of the kill, dismounted. Getting behind the leopard or cheetah, he then cunningly and swiftly pushed a hunk of meat through its hind legs towards its head. The animal, smelling this new lure, backed to investigate; and in that moment the man snatched his hare and leashed his leopard. It sounds like a job calling for extreme skill and speed.

A description of Kublai Khan's hunting with tigers cannot be better presented than in Marco Polo's own words.

"You must know that the great Khan has many leopards, all excellent for the chase and for catching game. He also has a large number of lynxes trained to hunt, and very good for the chase. He has many very big tigers too, much bigger than those of Babylon ... They are trained to take wild boars, wild oxen, bears, wild asses, stags, fallow deer and other beasts. And I assure you it is a splendid sight to see those tigers catch their quarries. When tigers are taken to the chase, each tiger is put in a cage on a cart, and a little dog with him. The reason they are placed in cages is that otherwise they would be too fierce and anxious to fall on the game, and it would be impossible to hold them. They have, moreover, to be led to the windward *(sic)* of the game, for if the latter scented them, they would flee and not wait for them to approach."

The Great Khan was an industrious hunter. He also had "a multitude of eagles, trained to catch wolves, foxes, deer and roes; and they take many of them. Those trained to catch wolves are remarkably big and powerful. For you may be sure there is not a wolf, however big, that can escape them."

(In a more extravagant vein Marco Polo wrote of an eagle, in Madagascar, so large "that he can with his talons carry an elephant into the air", and drop it for food!)

The Khan, though so enthusiastic a slaughterer, had very strict close seasons for his game. Indeed, if he had not, he would eventually have had none left. Nothing was allowed to be killed between March and October, the breeding season. "And who should transgress this order, would be made bitterly to rue it, for so the Great Khan has decreed. But I assure you his demands are so respected, that often enough hares and deer and the other animals I have mentioned come right up to people, and no one touches them or does them any harm."

Before we leave Peking let us move on a hundred years and look at the monastery of Paiens, a little way out of the city. Here the monks had an enclosed park, so big that it had "a high mountain" in the middle. This park was the home of a great number of monkeys and marmosets, and, rather oddly, the catalogue includes butterflies. The monkeys were believed to house the souls of dead noblemen: commoner souls being housed in commoner beasts. Those who had been great in human life must not be neglected now that they were in simian form. Consequently, living noblemen—no doubt bearing in mind what they must expect to come to—gave the monks enough money to feed their charges generously. The monks, it is true, benefited first. Every day, after they themselves had dined, the bountiful remains were put into gold vases to be carried to the park. There the almoner blew on a silver trumpet; and the monkeys, familiar with the sound and what it heralded, hurried to the feast.

In Europe we do not hear of tame tigers until the 17th century. The Moroccan Ambassador gave Louis XIV a tigress, and she was said to be "as gentle as a bitch". She was taken to St. Germain, and there led about among the Queen and her ladies, who caressed and played with this new exotic pet.

Now we see again the split mind so common in past ages in man's relationship with his animals. This tigress was treated as a familiar, a creature to be stroked and played with. But this did not save her from the eternal animal contests. She was put to fight a cow. One might well suppose that a cow stood no chance at all against a tiger. In this case the cow was belligerent and courageous above her kind. She defeated the tigress. That was not the end for her. Immediately she was faced with a lioness. Overcoming that, the poor brute then conquered in turn another lioness, another tiger, and yet another lion. By this time—it could not be otherwise—she was badly mauled: the skin was off one haunch, and she was lame. Mercilessly, her tormentors now let a wolf loose upon her. Only when the valiant, exhausted animal had beaten this too was she led out of the arena.

The tiger has never been as easy to domesticate as the lion; and few have allowed as much familiarity as did Louis XIV's tigress. Later in time there is record of two Bengal tigers belonging to a travellingshowman, and these, neither muzzled nor chained, used to play with their master and show him every sign of affection. Another showman took his tiger about attached by a cord to his (the owner's) waist; this animal, too, would lick his owner's hand and rub against him.

The famous Tippoo Sahib, Sultan of Mysore in the latter half of the 18th century, kept at the door of his palace two tigers held on silver chains. They are not the only tigers connected

with him! Remembering the mechanical lions that Bishop Liudprand described eight centuries earlier, it is fascinating to find
Tippoo Sahib being greatly entertained by "a life-sized musical
tiger" which, with appropriate snarls and growls, ate up a
British officer—fortunately, equally mechanical. This contraption had been built by a Frenchman: hence, presumably, the
nationality of the prey.

This Sultan kept many wild animals; and after his death
several of them, notably monkeys, were bought by the Museum
of Natural History, Paris.

While on the subject of tigers it may be mentioned that it
was believed right up to this century—and probably still is in
some corners of the world—that a tiger's whiskers, especially
when scalded, are highly poisonous, and make a very efficient
drink to end your enemy's life.

CHAPTER VIII

The French Court

For as far back as we can go wild animals have ranked as "status symbols" for those who kept them in their palaces, their great houses. And it was these nuclei of (particularly) lions and bears kept by the various rulers of Europe which—with a few to fall out by the wayside—were the seeds of the great zoological gardens of today.

We have seen our own start at Woodstock, under Henry III, and later we will follow its development. Now it is time to look at France.

The Zoo in that country has a long, intricate and stormy history. It is not easy to pinpoint its beginnings, because there had been an unbroken custom of keeping wild animals going right back to the amphitheatre games learned from the Romans. Indeed, these lasted longer here than in the city of their origin, where the influence of Christianity brought them sooner to an end.

As good a starting-point as anywhere is in 1333, the year Philippe VI bought a two-hundred-year old grange situated in the grounds of the Château de Louvre. This he converted into a *Hôtel des lions du Roi*. Here leopards as well as lions were kept, and this zoo lasted for forty-two years, until Charles V moved the entire collection to St. Pol.

By this time St. Pol was a splendid place, with thirteen gardens, and holding, besides, lions, boars, seals, porpoises and innumerable birds.

Charles V was passionately attached to birds. Or, to speak more truly, he would have said that he was. For no true bird-lover could really care to see caged birds in all of his rooms, as he kept them at the Château de Louvre. To be sure, the conception of cruelty in this respect was unlikely to enter into a fourteenth-century mind. According to his lights he did well by his little captives. They were housed, many of them, in gold and silver cages, jewel-studded.

It is an interesting digression that this King built on the edge of a wood at Vincennes a "splendid châlet", which he named *Manoir de Beauté*; and it was this house which his grandson was to give to his English mistress, Agnes Sorel. The gardens of this Manor were enhanced—at least in the eyes of Charles V—by caged nightingales hanging in the trees. Not content with these and his other caged birds, he also had in his palace an aviary full of nightingales. Presumably these poor prisoners sang, or there would have been no point in keeping them.

This caging of birds was a common practice. A young Duke of Burgundy is recorded as having in his room twenty-four cages of finches and siskins. Nor was the habit confined to the wealthy. According to their means, all the people of France liked to keep caged birds.

After the Louvre animals had been moved to St. Pol, the varieties of creatures kept there increased, and particularly under the next King, Charles VI, who was mad. His wife and the courtiers tried to distract him from his melancholy with new animals. He was given, among other curiosities, an albino goldfinch, a dancing bear, and a wolf which two boys had caught "with great difficulty".

This menagerie lasted until the end of the 15th century, and in the meantime Louis XI—taking a leaf out of our King's book—had announced that the upkeep of it was to be borne by the people of Paris and not by the Royal Purse.

There were animals still at Vincennes, which had been a deer-park at least since the twelfth century, when deer were sent over from England. These of course were for hunting. One has to remember that there would be a few wild animals—if only two or three—at every royal residence; and this makes a direct history confusing, as often the animals were moved about.

Henry VI of England's consort, it will be remembered, was Margaret of Anjou, whose father, René, Count of Anjou, owned the biggest menagerie in France. But while his daughter was installing—literally—new life into the Tower of London, René's own great menagerie was fading away. His animals moped and died. He did all that he could. He built better houses for them; still they did not thrive. This was scarcely surprising. However careful and well-intentioned owners or keepers were, the husbandry of great cats in captivity was an art that had not been mastered in fifteenth-century Europe.

The Anjou menagerie was not revived. René went to live in his estates in Provence, where he already had another, and smaller, collection of wild animals.

Meanwhile, his sister who was Queen of France (consort of Charles VII) and as great an animal-lover as himself, kept pets as varied as a wild goat, bustards, a porpoise and hares. It is only in the last hundred years or so that hares have gone out of favour as pets. All know that the poet Cowper owned one; and their history as companions goes back a very long way, for they were kept by early Greek and Roman ladies. The Queen of France bred from her hares, and her particular pets wore black velvet collars.

Her son Louis (later Louis XI), when he was a little boy, was given a lioness cub by his Uncle René. The child was so devoted to his pet that he insisted on its sleeping in an alcove in his bedroom. The cub was on a collar and chain. Unluckily there was a window above her sleeping-quarters, and one night she jumped out, and inadvertently hanged herself. Her heart-broken owner kept her skin.

This boy grew up to be fanatical about hunting. Often he hunted conventionally in the forest. At other times he let loose in the palace courtyard, it might be boars, foxes, hares, rabbits, even—most unlikely of all—hedgehogs, and hunted these. If it was raining and he did not wish to go out and get wet, he found his sport by releasing a lot of rats in his room, and setting cats to catch them. He also owned a leopard specially trained to hunt hares.

This mania for hunting or for watching animals fight each other runs deep and monotonous, monotonous through all the centuries...

But it is horrifying to read of another little Queen-Consort of France, Anne of Brittany, wife of Charles VIII, who when only sixteen years old found pleasure in putting asses and lions into an enclosure to "see them play and fight". One imagines there would not be much playing. Donkeys, contrary to popular opinion, are very courageous animals and will turn and attack their enemies. Long ago, children used to have an ass skin put over them in the belief that this would give them courage.

A far more terrible tale is told of a royal French child, considerably later in time. Louis XV reared a fawn, which of course became deeply attached to him. But when the deer became full grown the young King (he had succeeded to the Throne at five years old) had no more heart than to shoot at it. The wounded hind, remembering her master's kindness in the past, ran to him. He shoo'd it away, and shot at it until he had killed it. Somehow, that the trusting deer was a female makes the sickening story even worse.

But back to our fourteenth-century muttons.

The French nobility were all as "animal-minded" as the English nation of today are supposed to be. A French authority goes so far as to say that all the Princes of the family of the unbalanced Charles VI "showed a mental weakness in their overpowering love of animals". Especially this was the case with one of the Dukes of Berry. He owned several menageries and aviaries; and, besides, kept as in a zoo all kinds of dogs. This royal gentleman was captured by the English for a hostage in 1360. While he was a prisoner he fell in love with an English lady called Ursine. So enamoured of her was he that after he had returned to France, in memory of her he incorporated a bear into his coat-of-arms; and, what was more, wherever he went, he took a live bear with him!

Mad though Charles VI was, he passed a very pleasing law. At the time of Coronations (which then took place at Rheims) and also on the occasion when any Queen of France entered Paris for the first time, it became obligatory for all the very many bird-dealers to release four hundred of their birds. This will give some idea of the numbers of caged birds stocked. The law was in force for a long time. At the Coronation of Louis XI, all together, freed from a great net spread over the Pont-au-Change, over two thousand song-birds soared into freedom. Whether indeed these captives would have been able to survive and feed themselves is another matter.

Arising out of this, it became the custom at Notre Dame, during the Whitsunday Divine Office to release small birds in the Cathedral.

To move on to Henri II's time, it is to find Mary Queen of Scots as a child at the French Court: the only truly happy time in the whole of her tragic life. She and the royal children between them had, besides horses, ponies and hawks, over twenty dogs and numberless birds. At the Château at Blois they also kept tame bears. These were in the charge of a certain unfortunate lady called Madame Pillone, who had to keep them in her own house. Here they did so much damage that she was paid compensation.

By 1570 a collection of wild beasts was again at the Château de Louvre; kept there not for any pleasure to be gained in looking at them, but that, for entertainment, they might be put to fight with each other. For this purpose a vast arena was built in the gardens, capable of holding a thousand spectators. Catherine de Medici, mother of the King, now Charles IX (she who for the brief time his elder brother had reigned had been Mary Queen of Scots's mother-in-law), added such diversions as an echo and a maze. She also built new accommodation for the animals near to the arena.

The next King, Charles's younger brother, Henri III, increased the menagerie at the Louvre; but he also wiped it out, and for this reason. He had a dream—we know the very night of his dream, January 20th 1583—in which all the animals got loose and attacked him. A more sensible man might have concluded that he had indigestion, but Henri took his dream seriously, and he was heartily frightened. The very next day, after hearing Mass, he went down to the gardens with a harquebus and massacred every creature.

His successor, the Huguenot Henri IV (the romantic Henry of Navarre), who spent a good part of his reign campaigning against the Catholics, took everywhere with him on his expeditions a little "zoo" so small that it could all be carried on the back of one horse! It consisted of a big monkey called Robert, three smaller monkeys and a parrot. This little collection was presently to be enlarged—in every sense of the word—by the gift of an elephant. This animal arrived at Dieppe while Henri was besieging Noyon. It must have been a bitter disappointment to him that he could not immediately leave his post to see it; for this was the first elephant to land in France since the days of St. Louis IX, some three hundred years earlier.

Delighted though the King was with his elephant, he found that the cost of keeping it was excessive; and at the end of a year he offered it to Queen Elizabeth I of England who, he had been told, "greatly desired this animal".

Returning to Paris three years later, Henri took a great interest in the royal menageries. To Fontainebleau he brought animals especially for contests. More worthily, he built there a great aviary holding such varied birds as ostriches, herons, sea-gulls, peacocks, sheldrakes, pheasants, partridges, and cormorants trained to go fishing. Fish, both for food and sport, were necessary in large numbers; so he built fishponds.

The main royal menagerie was now at the Tuileries. A very strange present arrived here, given to the King by the Sultan Soliman, known as *Le Grand Seigneur*. It was an animal with "the head of a leopard and the body of a tiger". Presumably it was a hybrid between the two: there are instances of lions and tigers being crossed, but this is the only leopard-tiger hybrid I have heard about. It was a very fierce beast, and killed one of the keepers. The King therefore, it seems a little unsuitably, gave it to a travelling showman (a numerous species in those days): and he exhibited it in the Rue de la Harpe for two sous.

At the end of the 17th century the livestock from the Tuileries was sent to Vincennes; and after twenty or thirty years these in their turn went to Versailles. It may be mentioned in passing that, phoenix-like, a new zoo was to emerge again at Vincennes. Today, there is to be found there one of the finest zoological gardens of Europe, and the best in France.

As for the Versailles menagerie, that was so splendid and has so fascinating a history it must have a chapter to itself.

None of these many royal menageries was open to the public. Only privileged people might visit them, with the express permission of the sovereign. Louis XIV was to break this rule, and not, as we shall see, with very happy results.

But although the common people could not go to the royal menageries, they were not deprived of the sight of wild animals. The travelling showmen went everywhere up and down the country; and poor sorry beasts most of their charges must have been. Many of them did tricks, and in early days the showmen were allowed into Paris without paying the customary toll on condition of their making their monkeys perform,

Travelling showmen of all nationalities, wandering the known world, showed all sorts of animals: probably always monkeys, but also, according to their means, bears, boars, armadillos, lions, wolves, even an occasional elephant, and many other creatures. Besides these professional men, the public also had a chance to see the beasts destined for the menageries of Versailles, Chantilly and other private collections, as they made their sad walk from their native countries across Europe, the keepers charging for the privilege, and thus making a little on the side.

Before gentler tastes prevailed with the Renaissance, a favourite entertainment given by the travelling showmen was a wrestling match between a man and a lion: a spectacle that was to become popular again much later on, in the early eighteen-hundreds. Certainly, one wonders whether at least some of these beasts had not had their teeth and claws drawn, as in Roman times...

There are details of a travelling showman's lion which was exhibited at Fontainebleau before Louis XIV. This one without doubt had his teeth. He would "kiss" his master, who then put his finger in the lion's mouth. The culminating trick was the man putting his whole head into his beast's mouth. But Louis, having been told by somebody who had already seen him doing this, that beforehand the man went "pale as linen", ordered that this trick should not be performed in his presence.

(The man had reason to pale. A successor who did the same thing much later at Edmonton Fair "fell a victim to his rashness".)

So Louis was content to see simpler examples of submission. The lion stood up or lay down as he was told; he lifted up his feet, one after the other, on command. The courtiers greatly admired him; but it was admitted that at his feeding-time (he ate, by the way, twenty-five pounds of mutton a day) he was so ferocious the timid backed away. As one young lady wrote: "His roaring makes me feel I shall faint."

Such lions as these, and other show animals, were not usually caged as in later times, but led from place to place. Not quite like dogs, for greater precautions were taken. In a contemporary picture of a pair of lions being led through the steets of Constantinople it can be seen what safety measures were taken. The lions are attached to each other by a short chain from their collars. Three leading chains are used. One comes from the middle of the yoking chain, and this is held by a man walking in front of the lions. Two other men flank the lions, each holding a chain attached to the collar of the lion beside him; both these men hold in their free hands a stick. A fourth man brings up the rear, and he too has a stick.

Another picture shows a giraffe parading the streets. He wears a halter, and from the noseband depend reins which are taken down through two bands of rope tied round the giraffe's neck; the further end of these long reins is held by the keeper, and behind him goes another man with a stick. In the picture the giraffe is being beaten, which rather belies the remarks of a travelling Frenchman: "It is wonderful how they know how to treat these beasts so gently and make them perfectly tame."

CHAPTER IX

A Beautiful and Terrible Zoo

When that great Spaniard, Hernando Cortes (cunning to his own superiors as to the enemy), came in 1519 with a handful of men into Tenochtitlan, ancestor of what we now know as Mexico City, it was to find in Montezuma's capital a world of wealth and luxury beyond the dreams of the most imaginative. This is not the place to recount Cortes' conquest; but the entire fantastic expedition reads like a folk-legend, with Cortes unwittingly coming in the role of expected god—and a treacherous god he was to prove.

The city was difficult to approach. It was built on an island in the Lake of Mexico, and could be reached only by several narrow causeways. When the Spaniards entered they were dumbfounded by what they saw. Very good descriptions survive, both in letters from Cortes, and in a book written in his old age by one of his soldiers, Bernal Diaz.

Everything in Tenochtitlan was on a scale of luxury simply not to be found anywhere in the world today. Gold was as common to these Mexicans as brass to Benares; and they had craftsmen worthy to work the superlative metal. There was gold everywhere. Even the cloaks of the Emperor were woven with threads of pure gold. If we tend to think of this strange civilization as merely a barbaric one, with its sacrifices of hearts cut throbbing from living men, we have also to remember that Montezuma's standards of personal cleanliness were higher than any that we practise. He changed his clothes four times a day and, excepting his ceremonial robes, he never wore any garment a second time. Similarly, his towels and his dishes were used only once. (Great perks for courtiers at *that* Court!)

Fascinating as such details are, we are really only concerned with the zoo. It was, probably, the most magnificent one, as to surroundings, that has ever been. With its beautiful pavilions, palatial aviaries, sculptured dens, it was laid out in a great garden near to the Imperial Palace; and this garden was surrounded by other vast gardens. All were perfectly kept, and planted throughout with flowers, sweet-smelling shrubs, and many herbs. Indeed—if one may be forgiven for twisting words—it could be said to be also a botanical zoo, for every flower of the country was represented. A newcomer might have been surprised to see in all this extravagance of vegetation not a single fruit-tree, not a vegetable, nor any plant that could be eaten. The reason for this was that in Montezuma's view a plant that was in any way useful marred a garden laid out purely for pleasure.

These were gardens like gardens in the *Arabian Nights*. There were fountains; there were ten great fishponds, some of salt water, some of fresh, all paved about with marble; and on this splendid flooring strutted, preened, dozed innumerable aquatic birds. Around the ponds, here and there, were airy, ornate pavilions, each with a balcony "cunningly arranged", so that the Emperor and his many ladies, seeking shelter from the heat of the day, could watch the birds below.

The great splendour of Montezuma's zoo lay, as well as in its buildings, in its design. Nearly three hundred years were to pass after the conquering Spaniards' sacking of city, palace, beasts, birds, all, before men again had the idea of keeping wild animals in a setting that was both beautiful and natural—if a tamed naturalness—instead of laying out menageries on a geometric pattern as was for so long the convention.

The most striking feature in the zoo of Tenochtitlan was the vast aviary known as the Palace of Birds. The pillars upholding this palace, and the flagstones of it, were "all jasper, beautifully worked". The native Mexican birds can vie with any jewels for colour and vividness, and all were here. In the centre of this enormous aviary was a lake of sweet water. This—as for the fishponds—had meant engineering problems. The water of Mexico Lake, although it is inland, is salt. The fresh water had to be brought by aqueduct from neighbouring Chapoltepec.

The birds alone had three hundred people, men and women, to look after them. Some caught fish in the lake to feed their charges, the amount needed—and this gives some idea of the number of fish-eating birds alone—being two hundred and fifty pounds daily. Others went into the countryside solely to catch insects for food.

This numerous band of keepers of course kept the place clean, and cared in every way for the birds. At nesting-time they put up nests for them (one wonders why the birds were not trusted to build their own), and took care that nothing disturbed the brooding hens and, later, the fledgling chicks.

Moulting-time was a time of harvest. All the bright feathers were carefully gathered up; and indeed the keepers assisted by pulling out by hand some of the loose ones. These feathers were not wasted.

Next to the Palace of Birds was a special pavilion, which could almost be described as a factory. A very superior factory. The workers in these pleasant surroundings, and with these gorgeous raw materials, were ladies no less in rank than the many wives of Montezuma. Here, all made of feathers, with some embroidery, they fashioned garments like coats; and especially favoured for this work were the green feathers of the quetzal, that glorious green and red bird with its phenomenal yard-long tail-feathers of a brilliant green.

How beautiful must have been these "coats of many colours", vivid with blue and green and yellow and red, and all the jewel-like colours of the native birds. Coats—if we could have them today—to be truly gloried in, since nothing was killed to procure them. Not so may Madam glory in her leopard-skin or tiger coat: she should hide her head in shame to wear one...

When the birds died a natural death they were, if required, stuffed to form what we would now call an ornithological museum.

The next great building was the Palace of the Birds of Prey and, in the same construction, the apartments of the carnivorous wild animals. As the first Palace held only beautiful and harmless birds, so this one, as its name indicates, housed a very great number of flesh-eating birds, ranging in size from kestrels to eagles. The different species appear to have had quite modern types of enclosure, with an inner compartment as well as one open to the air.

The menu for the birds of prey was five hundred turkeys

daily. Turkeys may spell luxury and Christmas to us; but in those days they happened to be the cheapest meat in Mexico. Other kinds of poultry were also given.

Another three hundred people were in charge, not only of the birds of prey, but of the neighbouring beasts as well.

The cages of these were built below ground-level, but were roomy, light and well-ventilated. They were made of very thick planks strongly pegged together. Above each den was a sculptured representation of the living animal within. The fact that nearly all these animals bred in captivity argues that they were well-cared-for and reasonably content.

Now we come to the macabre side of this beautiful zoo. The lions and other great cats had a far more revolting diet than their feathered neighbours. True, they too had turkeys, other poultry, deer and dogs. But a good part of their sustenance was human flesh.

Indeed, it has been suggested that the Mexicans started keeping carnivorous beasts as a convenient method of disposing of this commodity, of which they had, owing to their religion, a great deal.

For the Mexicans worshipped an insatiable god. His name translated into English was—inappropriately—Hummingbird, and he had to have as sacrifices hearts cut from the living bodies of men. It followed that, to appease their god's perpetual appetite, the people of Tenochtitlan were constantly at war with their neighbours in order to get enough hearts.

But do not think that, with the heart cut out, then the whole body was given to the beasts. No. The Mexicans themselves ate the limbs, and only the torsos were fed to the zoo.

Before the final overthrow of Tenochtitlan, many of Cortes' soldiers were to suffer the fate of being sacrificed to Hummingbird; and all lived their days in that luxurious and lovely city in dread of it ...

Near to the carnivores' apartments were the enclosures for the vegetarian animals, such as deer, llamas, vicunas (these latter already domesticated) and the "rare Mexican bull". This, presumably, was a near relation to, if not precisely, the North American Bison.

Almost every kind of reptile was also to be seen in this zoo. The snakes were kept either in big troughs half-filled with muddy water, or else in long chest-like enclosures, and supplied with down and feathers to cover and keep warm their eggs. The snakes, too, got a share of human meat; but chiefly they were fed on dogs.

This whole wonderful menagerie and gardens had originally been planned purely for pleasure and to enhance the prestige of the Emperors of Mexico. Only later was there a certain practical side to it—apart from the convenient disposal of corpses. By the time the Spaniards arrived several of the animals were specifically reared, either to be hunted or to be used for sacrifices: to lesser gods than Hummingbird, and these the priests would pick out. The Mexicans had a use, besides, for furs, which they needed both for clothing and for rugs.

Although the creatures bred well in captivity, Montezuma and his predecessors did not rely on this for keeping up the zoo population. There were yearly levies on the different countries under the Empire, by which they had to send to Tenochtitlan a quota of beasts and birds.

There was no shortage of wild animals. In the markets they waited to be bought, chained up and wearing collars, no different in this respect from the slaves beside them also awaiting purchase.

The Mexicans truly admired both their birds and their animals. Craftsmen came to the Palace gardens and modelled from life in pure gold. To think of them! Gold models of pumas, cheetahs, lizards, ducks, all kinds of birds and beasts "beautifully worked and perfect imitations". The conquistadores brought back many; and though a great part of their treasure was lost in the waters of the lake in the first great rout, yet some came through in safety to reach Spain at last. What happened to them? Nearly all these lovely irreplaceable works of art were melted down for the sake of their gold...

There was yet another "palace" in the zoo of Tenochtitlan: a very different one. Here Montezuma, who had a depraved taste in such matters, kept a large collection of human monsters: freaks such as dwarfs, hunchbacks, albinos, giants and worse; and people with deformities. All these, as though they had been different species of beasts, were divided according to their type of monstrosity or deformity, and each kind, both men and women, kept, with their guards, in separate apartments. For instance, there was a special room for albinos: as Cortes describes them, "men, women and children, who have been white since their birth, face, body, hair, eyebrows and eyelashes."

As for the deformed, these unfortunates were of particular and bizarre interest to Montezuma. He had them especially sought for, and evidently paid well for any brought to him. The horrible fact is—or certainly was believed to be so by the Spaniards—that parents, seeing good money to be made, would purposely deform their helpless infants; and then, when they were a little older, bring them to the Emperor's collection.

That at Tenochtitlan was not the only menagerie in Mexico. There was a notable one at Tezuco, a town considered the "scientific capital" of the Empire. This was intended as a complete living museum of natural history. Such animals as it was not possible to procure alive were represented by gold statuettes; and to show the colour and, as it were, the texture of the missing animal, if its hair had been obtainable they exhibited tapestries woven from this "to complete, by exact representations ... those animals which one could not observe living."

Montezuma's magnificent zoo at Tenochtitlan perished when Cortes and his men, after a period of peace when they lived and watched inside the city, attacked and eventually sacked it. It was set alight in the first raid, but survived that; and many of the Spaniards' bodies went—as they had often feared—to feed those great snarling beasts which, in life, they had admired ...

Cortes and his soldiers brought back to Spain more than golden animals. They returned with living trophy: turkeys, guinea-pigs, llamas, alpacas and vicunas. And with these last animals the Spanish kingdom made its first serious effort to acclimatize creatures from a far country.

CHAPTER X

Chantilly and Vineuil

Chantilly was the property of the de Montmorency family until Louis XIII confiscated it when the owner rebelled against him in 1632. But after the King's death, eleven years later, Charlotte de Montmorency, who was the mother of the renowned soldier known to history as the Great Condé, was allowed to return.

It was under the Condés that Chantilly became a menagerie that rivalled and eventually, for a time, suprassed that at Versailles. Not immediately. There came the troubles of the Fronde rebellion when Condé, beaten by the royalist, Cardinal Mazarin, was forced in his turn to abandon his estates at Chantilly. The conquerors, not content with exiling the owner, laid waste the menagerie, killing all the animals—at that time chiefly deer and domestic creatures—and the great number of birds of many species. Not even the fish in the ponds were spared.

Here is no place to be concerned with the details of French political history. It is enough to say that seven years later Condé was permitted to return to Chantilly on condition of his holding no public office. Thus, this energetic and brilliant man found himself with much time on his hands before he was eventually restored to favour and once again led the French army. That was not for nine years, and during this long period of forced retirement the great General created a new and a far more magnificent menagerie.

When Condé finally retired from soldiering in 1675, he continued, with the help of his son, as enthusiastic as himself, to improve and to add to his zoo. He needed more land to implement his plans; although the menagerie was already so large that it stretched outside the original park of Chantilly onto part of his property near the village of Vineuil.

Adjoining was a certain fairly small estate, all enclosed by a wall; and this seemed to Condé ideal for his purpose. He tried to buy it. Unfortunately, the owner refused to sell. The Great Condé, never content with defeat, was determined to drive the owner to reconsider his decision. He chose an original method.

He ordered his gamekeepers and hunters to round up and catch alive a great pack of foxes and cubs, numbering three or four hundred, the biggest collection of these animals (as our chronicler remarks) that "without doubt was ever seen in the memory of man". He did not, like Sampson of old against the Philistines, tie them in pairs with burning brands on their tails: he simply let them all loose over the wall of the coveted estate. Since this was chiefly kept for game, the sheer quantity of foxes did tremendous damage.

Condé did not win this battle, however, The owner of the ravaged land happened to be a private secretary to the King; and he complained bitterly to his royal master. Louis XIV, though he may have been amused by the ingenuity of the ruse, upheld his secretary's rights, and ordered Condé to remove every fox and, further, to make reparation for all the harm they had done.

Condé had no choice but to comply. He had to be content with enlarging his menagerie around Vineuil. Thus it comes about that though Chantilly and Vineuil are sometimes referred to as if they were separate menageries, in fact they were virtually one.

After the Great Condé's death, his son, and his grandson after him, and more Condés after that, cared for, loved, and improved this great menagerie.

In the son's day there were five courts for animals. Each court had a name, though its title had nothing to do with the inmates. They were named, rather quaintly, after the Fables of La Fontaine—who, of course, was alive at that time. One, for instance, was called *The Jay in Peacock's Feathers;* and these words were inscribed in gold on a slab of black marble. The characters in the fable, cast in lead and painted, were to be seen on rocks inside the court.

At this time there were more birds than anything else in the Chantilly zoo; and it was not until the Great Condé's grandson's time that the first lions and tigers were brought there. Fine new buildings were put up to house them; and very modern they sound. There was both a kitchen and a bakehouse attached to the living quarters; as well as a special apartment to keep lion-cubs being reared by a bitch.

The Duchess of Berry was very amused to see, at a fête given at Chantilly in her honour, a full-grown lion still living with the bitch who had reared him. There are many tales of lasting friendships between lions and dogs; but in this particular case, sad to say, the lion was later to kill his foster-mother.

During this fête a "big and very beautiful" tiger escaped. As Saint-Simon remarks in his *Memoirs: "On peut juger de l'effroi et de l'inquiétude de toute cette cour rassemblée."* All was well. The tiger's keeper ran after him and led him back to his cage, without his having done the least harm to anyone except scaring the onlookers half out of their wits!

Among the improvements of later years was the substitution of iron railings for wooden ones between all the courts and cages.

Among the great variety of animals—which, however, did not include either an elephant or a rhinoceros—was a family of white deer. Such animals (even if not albinos) are not a true species, but what is known as a white phase; possibly caused by inbreeding, and to be found mostly in fallow or axis deer.

It is interesting to read of the method by which these white deer—and probably other animals—were moved from one part of the park to another. A high canvas corridor was erected between the two enclosures, and the deer driven down this to their new home.

One of the Condés tried to emulate the Roman Emperor Heliogabalus by putting his deer to harness. It was evidently not a success, since it is recorded that he drove them only *"un instant"*.

Shortly before the Revolution two reindeer arrived, male and female, a gift from the King of Sweden. He had sent three, but one died on the way. They were accompanied by a Lapp man and two Lapp women. It seems odd that for their home these people (who remained to look after the reindeer) were given the enclosure originally intended for beavers. The reindeer did not flourish. Within four months the second male died, and, there now being so little to do, the two Lapland women returned home.

One of the great glories of Chantilly was its waterways and ponds. There were fish innumerable: of carp forty thousand "of all possible colours and very tame". Some were as much as two feet long. There was also a crocodile, who came to the shore when he was called, and enjoyed having his keeper scratch him on the underneath of his lower jaw.

One of the lakes was enclosed, and in this was kept a pair of wild swans which had had their flying pinions cut so that they could not escape. Very great interest was roused by these birds. Not merely for their beauty, grace, size, whiteness; but because it began to be rumoured through Chantilly, and the rumour spread to Paris twenty-six miles away, that these two swans sang, as did the classic swans of old.

Swan song is part of our language now, and we do not usually stop to consider how the expression arose. Everyone knows that it is a song of departure. A swan was believed to sing only at the approach of death. The great naturalist, Pliny, did not believe this. He wrote: "Some say that the Swans sing lamentably just before their death; but untruly, I suppose, for my experience with several has shown the contrary."

Socrates had thought differently; and he also believed that men were quite mistaken in thinking that the swans' song before dying was for grief.

As he wrote in *The Phaedo:* "Because of the fear that men have of death, they speak falsely of the swans, saying that when they are singing their last song, they are wailing aloud with sorrow at having to die. But men forget that no bird sings when it is hungry or cold or suffers any pain, not even the nightingale or the swallow or the hoopoe, and these are birds, which, they say, sing long laments for grief. Therefore neither these birds nor the swans sing for grief, it seems to me. On the contrary the swans, I believe, as sacred to Apollo have a prophetic power, and, having foreknowledge of the good things they will find in the next world, on the day of their death they sing and rejoice much more than in any of the days gone before it . . ."

However this may be, interest in the Chantilly swans grew enormously, and the *savants* of Paris were agog to know whether it was indeed true that the swans were singing and, if they were, what the song sounded like.

A Canon of St. Geneviève, one Antoine Mongez, travelled to

Chantilly to learn the truth. The swans sang for him, and he was "transported". He wrote a report of the event, which was presently read out before the Academy of Sciences "to great applause". It was also read before another learned body who were equally enthusiastic.

Here is Mongez' description of the swan song.

The male sang the notes *mi, fa,* and the female *re, mi* in an alternate chant. "Although their song has some resemblance, in the qualitiy of the sound, to the tearing cry of the peacock, it does not fail to please the ear ... It is astonishing that this song should be agreeable, for it is so piercing that one can hear it of an evening from the Apremont hillock, one league from the menagerie."

Other people, too, heard these swans, and all were "surprised by the loudness and the sweetness" of their song.

The owner of the swans, the Prince of Condé, very naturally wished to hear for himself these birds of his which had so excited the learned world of Paris. Accompanied by Canon Mongez and two members of the Academy of Sciences, he went to the swans' enclosure. But on this occasion the swans remained silent.

The professors and Canon Mongez consulted together. A great man like the Prince, and he the owner too, ought not to be disappointed. One of the party then remarked that it was well known that swans only sang as a sign of victory or from a "lively emotion". The suggestion was quickly made that a tame swan should be put in the wild swans' pond: the wild swans, being aggressive, would not tolerate this.

As had been foreseen, the unfortunate and blameless intruder was immediately attacked and killed. After that, sure enough, the swans sang!

A celebrated naturalist of the day, Valmont de Bomare, in his *Dictionary of Natural History,* was far less enthusiastic about this matter. He wrote:

"The wild swan has a voice, but what voice? A piercing cry ... When the male and female cry together, the ear sensitively distinguishes a sort of sharp and disagreeable carillon ... The naturalist cannot say what is untrue ... If, among the moderns, someone pretends to have heard with his own ears that the swan in question has a melodious song, one must reply that the blind man of Cheselden has at least as much right and gains as much pleasure as if he were to interpret the colour scarlet when he hears the word trumpet ... I have related what I have seen, what I have heard, and I avow that here is on my part neither ill-humour nor deference."

The French Revolution, that holocaust at the cross-roads of modern European history, destroyed Chantilly, as it destroyed the menagerie at Versailles and so much else.

Three days before the fall of the Bastille on that memorable 14th July 1789 the Prince of Condé and his son fled France to safety. As so many in like case, he believed his exile would be short.

No Condé came back to Chantilly for twenty-five years.

Even at the time of the Prince's flight, the menagerie at Chantilly was much depleted and could not compare with the earlier days of its grandeur.

It was not until three years later that the property was finally confiscated by the new Republic. In the meantime, through correspondence, the Prince had managed to sell some of the remaining animals in order to meet expenses and to pay bills.

On 15th August 1792, at six o'clock in the evening, a detachment of the National Guard, as it happened the famous batallion of Récollets, *les Marseillais,* ransacked Chantilly. Before they opened their attack on both the Château and the menagerie they killed an unlucky miller who got in their way, and marched into the estate with his head stuck up on a pike. It was indeed a grisly warning. The terrified Condé servants, both indoor and outdoor, fled, and so did the steward (or supervisor) of the menagerie.

The field having been thus taken, the soldiers dispersed for the night. When morning came they began their depredations in earnest. First, they broke everything in the Château that could be broken, smashing windows, destroying furniture, china, mirrors, slashing tapestries and curtains ... After that, they began the slaughter of the animals and the birds. The tiger, the only truly ferocious animal in the menagerie, was spared, not from any pity or admiration, but because no one dared to try to shoot him even with a cannon, for fear of missing and merely breaking open the cage. This massacre went on, with intermissions, for several days; and eventually there were left only, besides the tiger, a wild sheep, a large monkey and a civet-cat; and of the many, many birds only two eagles and five peacocks.

A month later the authorities ordered that these pitiful remnants of a great menagerie were also to be killed. This was done. The two eagles alone escaped; their lives were begged for by a certain Sieur who—rather surprisingly—was allowed to take them away to keep at his own expense.

Thus ended, after more than a hundred years, the splendid zoological gardens of Chantilly and Vineuil.

A rather sad little footnote is that, in 1818, the site was sold to a bleacher and cloth manufacturer, and the house built there was named the *Ménagerie de Chantilly*. It was still standing at the end of last century.

CHAPTER XI

Notable Exhibits

1

What is believed to be the first orang-utan to have arrived in Europe came from Angola in 1640 to the menagerie of Frederick Henry of Nassau, a son of William the Silent. It was described by the Dutch doctor, Nicholas Tulp, as an "Indian satyr".

No other orang-utan was seen in Holland for more than a hundred years. Again it was a Prince of Orange who had the privilege of owning it. He had two residences with zoos attached to them: the *Groote Loo* and the *Kleine Loo*. It was at the latter that he kept this orang-utan, a female. She was very gentle and affectionate; and only when no one was with her did she fall out of spirits, and could be heard moaning to herself.

When modern zoo-keepers read of her diet, they will probably not be astonished that she did not live very long. She would eat, the record says, almost anything, and this included boiled or roast meat or fish. These dishes she ate like a human, with spoon and fork; and—also humanlike!—she very much enjoyed washing them down with a glass of wine. Tantalizingly, we are told, with no instances given, that "often she showed signs of an intelligence more than animal".

Whether or not her diet was partly to blame (and the climate must have been a factor), her liveliness turned to quietness, and she became thin and wasted. By the end of a year she was dead.

This was not quite the end of her story. Her body had previously been promised to the wife of the Russian Ambassador to The Hague, the Princess Amélie Galitzine. She happened to be at Münster when the orang-utan died, and by the time her letter arrived claiming the corpse, the Director of the *Kleine Loo* Zoo, who had already pickled it in spirits, refused to hand it over.

A long and tart correspondence followed; but the Princess, who had doubtless hoped to have the ape stuffed, lost the battle.

Later, Napoleon's Josephine kept an orang-utan at Malmaison, which used to sit and eat at her table, wearing a coat.

Another unusual animal was the rhinoceros that belonged to Manuel I of Portugal: a king who on grand occasions liked to parade through Lisbon with either an elephant or a rhinoceros walking before the horse on which he was mounted.

Manuel's rhinoceros is the very one depicted in the famous engraving by Albrecht Dürer. It was not, however, done from life, but from a drawing by another artist who sent his sketch to Dürer. The latter might have been curious enough to travel to Lisbon to see it if the rhinoceros had not already been on the brink of departure. Manuel was sending it as a present to the Pope, Leo X.

The animal travelled by sea, and the ship put in at Marseilles. This was the year 1517, and such beasts as elephants and rhinos were rare in Europe. Indeed, it was only since Vasco da Gama some twenty years earlier had discovered the Cape route to India that these great creatures had been seen in Portugal since the fall of the Roman Empire. Few had been seen elsewhere in Europe; although da Gama's discovery was opening up the trade for wild animals both from India and Asia.

It so happened that the King of France, François I, was at Marseilles when this ship with the Pope's rhinoceros aboard arrived. His Majesty requested the Master to allow the animal ashore so that the townspeople might see so extraordinary a beast. This was done, and the rhino caused "great excitement". As a reward for thus obliging him the King presented the Master of the ship with a fine horse complete with harness and trappings, and five hundred golden crowns besides.

This splendid gift proved useless. Off Genoa the ship ran into a great storm, and was lost with all hands. The rhinoceros of course perished too; but its body was washed ashore. This was stuffed and, instead of the living beast, was sent to His Holiness in Rome.

Pope Leo X must have been bitterly disappointed. He was very interested in wild animals, and during his papacy the Vatican menagerie was at its best. (For Popes, like Kings, needed this symbol of grandeur).

The rhinoceros had not been Manuel's first gift. In honour of Leo's election as Pope he had sent him, among other presents, an elephant and an ounce.

This elephant did not behave very well. After the Pope's solemn public entry into Rome, His Holiness sat in a window to see the people and to be seen. As the elephant was led by, he did as he had been taught to do: he went down on his knees three times in homage. Then his little wicked eye fell upon a tub of water. He sucked it up, turned and showered the crowd and the Pope alike. Leo must have been a true animal-lover. Instead of being angry and feeling his dignity had been lowered, he was much amused; and the scene, we are told, greatly delighted him.

This elephant, so great a novelty, was to rouse tremendous enthusiasm. He had his portrait painted by many artists, and poets wrote verses to him.

It was long believed that elephants and rhinoceroses have a natural antipathy towards each other as dogs and cats have: particularly on the elephant's side.

Manuel I decided to find out. He chose a street, and had both ends of it blocked before turning loose in it a rhinoceros and an elephant with a man on his neck. An unenviable ride, certainly.

The animals chased each other; and presently the elephant was in such a state of terror and so desperate to escape from his enemy that he charged full at a large window which was protected by iron bars eight inches in circumference. His weight and impetus crashed these and he scrambled through the wreckage to safety. His less fortunate rider was swept off his back in the turmoil, and could hardly have escaped, at best, severe bruising. The story ends abruptly at this point, so his fate is unknown. One is left wondering, too, where the elephant found himself on the other side of the heavily barred window.

Though this encounter proved the truth of a natural enmity, on a much later occasion when an elephant belonging to Louis XVI was confronted with a rhino, this time with a stout fence between them, neither animal showed the slightest interest.

For long elephants remained a tremendous curiosity. (Even today when we are used to them, in pictures if not in the flesh, they are awe-inspiring.) When one was exhibited at the Fair at St. Germain in 1770, it was the first to have been seen in France for more than a hundred years. The Parisians flocked to look at it.

This Fair, incidentally, exhibited what we would call a circus: there were performing pigeons, dogs, monkeys. Of the latter, in one "turn" the monkeys rode big dogs, doing, if not precisely *haute école,* at least exercising "horsemanship in a surprising manner".

The first rhinoceros ever to be seen in Holland arrived there in the middle of the 18th century, brought in by a Dutch sea-captain who quickly sold it to a travelling showman. This animal, an eight-year old female from Assam was "the great curiosity of all Europe." Her owner seems to have known better how to care for her than the orang-utan's keepers knew how to care for their precious charge. Her daily diet was sixty pounds of hay and twenty pounds of bread, besides what the admiring public gave her. As for drink, she got through fourteen buckets of water in the day; and when on show drank wine and beer. (It was common to give exotic beasts spirituous liquors: the odd thing is that they took to them so readily.) She was said to enjoy tobacco too; the owner used to blow smoke into her nostrils to prove it. Great care was taken of her hide: it was frequently greased with fish-oil to prevent chapping and cracked skin: complaints prevalent in elephants and rhinoceroses.

It is interesting to compare this rhinoceros' diet with the more elaborate one given in captivity today. I am indebted to the Director of the Bristol Zoo for the following rhinoceros menu for one animal. Every day 4 lbs cattle grazing nuts, 1½ lbs flaked maize, 56 lbs carrots and mangolds, 76 lbs lucerne or clover, and as much elm or evergreen oak as they will eat. Besides, once a week this is supplemented with 4 lbs linseed, 1½ lbs crushed oats and the same of bran, 56 lbs of kale, and an eighth of a pint of codliver-oil put on the grazing nuts; finally 2 lbs of salt a week.

As for the oiling against cracked skin, this is not necessary if the animal is washed and kept clean. Sometimes vaseline is put round the eyes, and some zoos put vaseline round the toe-nails. The habit has not quite died out. In Colombo Zoo, for instance, the elephants have their hides oiled.

But to return to our 18th century rhinoceros.

She travelled Europe in a cage placed on a strong dray, the whole so heavy that it required twenty horses to pull it.

Eventually she arrived at Versailles, where the Court gaped in admiration and wonder.

One must remember, and keep on remembering, how *strange* these rarer animals were, unbelievably weird and wonderful. As wonderful as any moon-rock in our day and, being living, far, far more fascinating. No rhinoceros had set foot in France for well over two hundred years: not since the ill-fated one landed at Marseilles on its journey to Pope Leo X.

Louis XV wanted to buy her; but even he recoiled from the price. The showman knew he had a money-spinner, and he asked 100,000 crowns.

From Versailles he moved on to St. Germain, and there all Paris ran to look at the marvel. All who came were offered engravings of the beast at thirty sous; and also a thirty-four-page booklet on her nature and history. This had been written, anonymously, by a librarian at the Sorbonne. A brisk trade was done in both picture and literature; and in no time this ugly prehistoric-looking animal was absolutely the rage. Even fashions were named after her: styles advertized *à la rhinocéros,* ribbons the same. As a lady named only as Countess Dash was to write: "This wretched animal intruded everywhere, everything was *à la rhinocéros.*" The creature's portrait was painted by a well-known artist, and exhibited at the Salon the following year.

She went on in due course to Italy; and the Venetians received her with nearly as much enthusiasm as the Parisians. She was taken to all the masked carnivals; and certainly must have added to the gaiety and interest of these events. Imagine a rhinoceros in, say, the ballroom of the Savoy Hotel! Her portrait was engraved on a medal, for people to buy. She was also painted, and this picture found its way to the National Gallery in London.

The Parisians always welcomed unusual animals in their midst. There was exactly the same furore as there had been over the rhinoceros when a giraffe arrived seventy or eighty years later. No wonder! This was the first giraffe ever to be seen in France. Indeed, she was "the great event of all the countries".

A two-year old female, she was a present from the Pasha of

Egypt to the King of France, Charles X. She was sent by sea from Alexandria; and every precaution was taken for her health. Tied around her lengthy neck (she stood eleven foot, six inches) was a parchment upon which had been written several verses from the Koran: this was to protect her from all kinds of illness, but particularly those caused by witchcraft and enchantment. Three cows travelled with her that she might have the benefit of their milk. (Considering her age, this seems a little strange.) Four Arabs came to look after her.

Although she arrived in Marseilles in November, she did not reach Paris till June of the following year, 1827. This delay is easily explained. She would have to do the rest of the journey on foot, and this in winter time was obviously most unsuitable for a valuable animal accustomed to a hot country.

On her eventual arrival at the capital she was the talk of the day. Like the rhinoceros before her, Fashion took her up, so that ladies wore a dress described as *à la giraffe*; or a hat or a comb similarly named. Songs were written about her, and objects called after her. One could buy models of her, either in plain earthenware or with a light inside. For smaller, cheaper souvenirs there were bronze medals.

This giraffe happily survived, and lived in the *Jardin des Plantes* for twenty years.

The same Pasha, Mohammed Ali, gave a giraffe in the same year to George IV. As far as is known, this is the first giraffe ever to come into England. She was sent to Windsor, but unfortunately she had finished her journey in bad condition, and did not live long.

About ten years later four more giraffes arrived to be on show to admiring visitors in the young London Zoo.

2

To most people a white elephant probably brings to mind jumble sales rather than animals. Few probably have seen a white elephant. They do exist. Some are albinos; many others are very pale in colour and thus pass for white.

The earliest white elephant I have read of lived in Siam in 1636. It was one of six thousand belonging to the Royal Palace. Six thousand elephants, and caparisoned elephants at that! The imagination can scarcely visualize so magnificent a sight. This single white one was considered so special and so valuable that it was in the care of no ordinary elephant-keeper, but of so grand a person as one of the Princes of the Blood.

The next account comes from the Frenchman, Père Tachard, priest and traveller, writing about 1736.

"In a country house belonging to the King, situated upon the river about a league from Siam, I saw a small white elephant, which was destined to be the successor to the one in the Palace, which is said to be three hundred years old. This little elephant is somewhat larger than an ox, and is attended by many mandarins; and out of respect to him, his mother and aunt are kept along with him."

Here, as everywhere, there were contests. Père Tachard watched a fight between three elephants and a tiger in an arena enclosed by bamboos. The tiger, already at the disadvantage of three to one, and three massive opponents, was at first also handicapped by two men holding two cords attached to it. One elephant hit the tiger so hard with his trunk that the animal "lay as if dead". It was then freed from the cords. The only good thing to be said for this contest was, that when it seemed certain the tiger would be killed, the fight was stopped.

Another, and more famous Frenchman, Buffon, whose great *Natural History* was published in the mid-18th century, tells that the white elephant was considered so peerless a beast that the only human being before whom it must bow the knee was the Emperor himself; and the Emperor always returned the salute. (This was an honour not accorded to human beings.) In Sian, Laos and Pegu, if not in Siam, it was believed that these huge rare animals held the deified souls of past Indian* Emperors.

It hardly needs to be said that the white elephants, unlike their more ordinary brethren, were never made to do any work. Their life was one of luxury, and—as Buffon says— they were "flattered, but not corrupted". He goes on to add, rather sourly:

* India was a loose term for much of the eastern world.

"This circumstance alone should be sufficient to convince the Indians that these animals are not endowed with human souls."

Two English travellers to Bangkok in 1822 were so fortunate as to see six white elephants. These were definitely albinos. They were treated with awe and reverence, since Vishnu chooses white elephants in which to be reincarnated. Their tusks were banded with rings of gold, and across their foreheads they wore a gold circlet; on their backs were rugs of velvet. Each of these elephants had his own stable, with ten men appointed to look after him. Each had another attendant too in the form of an albino monkey. These creatures were also sacred; and were given to the elephants, not for company, but as a living talisman to protect them from all sickness.

Forty-five years later there was only one sacred elephant at Bangkok. This was not an albino, but a genuinely pale one. It too was heavily decorated: with gold bracelets, a gold collar, and charms and precious stones. Its food was served to it on enormous platters of engraved "precious metal"; and its water waited in magnificent silver vessels.

It is not out of place to mention here that in Japan albino horses used to be sacred.

As well as white elephants there are also, though as rare if not rarer, red elephants. In the procession of the King of Pegu (as described by a Dutch traveller in 1711) these were led in front of four white elephants. In spite of this precedence, they were evidently not quite so highly revered as the whites because, although caparisoned alike in "silk and gold stuff", the white elephants had the distinction of having their trappings embroidered with precious stones, and their "tusks covered with rubies".

CHAPTER XII

The Story of Woira

It will be remembered that in the Chantilly menagerie there was a lion living with the bitch which had reared him, and which afterwards he was to kill. Against this, there are several instances of lasting friendships between lions and dogs.

The most moving concerns the lion Woira who, born in his native land, lived most of his life at Versailles.

Before telling his story we will look at some earlier instances of unusual companionship.

It was often chance that, in the first place, made friendship between a dog and a lion, or a dog and a tiger.

A pleasing account comes from Morocco. It was recorded by the envoy of the French King, Henri IV, who was there in the year 1605. The keeper of the Moroccan lion-house was a Christian slave; and among the several lions in his charge the envoy, Maquet by name, was surprised to see a dog wandering in perfect safety. He questioned the man, who then told him the full tale of how the dog came to be there.

It was quite a common custom, even up to the 18th century, to feed carnivorous beasts on live dogs; and this one in the Moroccan lions' den had originally been intended to form part of the occupants' dinner. As soon as he had been put in, the oldest lion, who was the acknowledged leader, took the dog between his paws and started, catlike, to play with him before devouring him. The dog surely must have been a puppy (if a big one) not to have realized his danger and imminent death; for, far from being terrified, as one would expect, he appears to have played back, and while doing this began gently scratching with his teeth at a gall below the lion's throat. This sensation eased the lion, and gave him so much pleasure that, not only did he not harm the dog, but from thenceforward he took him under his protection, so that none of the other lions dared to hurt their leader's favourite.

When M. Maquet saw this dog, he had already lived among the lions for seven years.

The slave further told M. Maquet that when the lions fought over their food, the dog became so distressed that he tried to separate them. They paid no more attention to this small antagonist than to the buzzing of a fly; so, when his growls and snarls had failed, he sat down and howled loudly. For some reason this howling always frightened the lions, and they would then stop their fighting. The dog's own particular lion would allow his friend actually to take meat out of his jaws.

There is a very similar story about a tiger in the Schönbrunn Zoo in 1806.

This Bengal male suffered with sore eyes. In the belief that the hot blood of living flesh would ease his complaint, he was given, instead of the usual butcher's meat, live prey. One of these victims was a little bitch. At the time she was put into the cage, the tiger was lying down with his head on his forepaws. Evidently his eyes were paining him, and he was not hungry. At first the dog was terrified. Then, since the tiger did not move, she overcame her fear, crept up to him, and presently began to lick his running eyes. This gave relief to the tiger; and soon, instead of merely accepting her ministrations, he for his part began to lick and caress her. Her fear quite gone, the bitch spent all her time, off and on, licking at the sore eyes until, in only a few days, they were quite healed.

It is nice to be able to say that the tiger kept his gratitude, and continued to love the little dog so much that he would always allow her to feed first, even though she greedily, if naturally, took the best pieces. When they romped she could bite him, and he was never anything but gentle.

When these dog companions died, it was often difficult to introduce a new one; but it was usually thought worth trying since the bereaved beasts pined and went off their food.

One of the oddest stories of strange bedfellows concerns an eagle housed in the Museum of Natural History in Paris. This was about 1784. The great bird was moping and refusing its food. The keepers decided that the only hope of encouraging its appetite and so preventing it from dying, was to give it living prey. The victim chosen was an "English cock". He was put into the cage, and all stood round, hopefully waiting for the eagle to pounce. Instead, the eagle quite slowly approached the cock, looked him all over, and then—to the amazement of the spectators—spread a wing protectively over the smaller bird; and thus they walked together about the large cage.

The cock remained with the eagle, and from thenceforward it recovered its appetite for the usual dead meat, and was very soon completely restored to health. Simply, it had been moping for companionship. As our French author remarks: *"Chose curieuse et combien instructive!"*

But now to the tale of Woira.

At first he was the pet of a M. Pelletan, who was the Director of the French *Compagnie d'Afrique,* at Senegal. This cub, at three or four months old, was given to him in the year 1787. M. Pelletan was a true animal-lover, and he had many pets of different species, all of which lived in his house with him in perfect freedom. His pets were certainly of wide variety. We are told they were "horses, sheep, dogs, cats, monkeys, ostriches, geese, ducks, turkeys, hens, parrots", and now of course the little lion.

In the cool nights all these assorted creatures slept in the stables huddled together. The negroes joined in too for the warmth, and in this delightful hugger-mugger of heat, softness and comfort there was never any growling or dissension of any kind.

One evening when Woira came in to go to bed he found that his special place was occupied by a bitch which had just given birth to two puppies. Far from being annoyed at being thus displaced, the then eight-months-old Woira was greatly interested in these additions. He had not much chance at that moment to satisfy his curiosity, and probably he was growled at by the bitch.

With the passing of the days, so his interest grew. Whenever their mother left the puppies Woira stood guard over them. Not only that. Although he was so very much bigger, he caressed them with great gentleness. The bitch, for her part, while she did not mind seeing her pups between the lion's paws, soon shoo'd him off when she wanted to suckle them. To do this, she might snarl and show her teeth; but Woira never retaliated;

he simply good-naturedly retired until he could resume his own sort of nursing.

One of the puppies died, and Woira became even fonder of the remaining one. It was older now, and he never left it. These two ill-assorted beasts, a great cat and a little dog, played together incessantly; and the little dog could do whatever he liked with Woira, even nipping him in play till the blood came. The bitch, who was rather elderly, disapproved of so much romping, especially as pup and cub followed her about as they did their gambolling. Presently she was growling at the pair and chasing them away.

The dog loved the lion as much as Woira loved him. If they were separated both howled till they were reunited. At night the dog slept against Woira's stomach.

Woira seems to have been one of those rare perfect animals (as saints among men are rare). He was as charming to his master as to his canine friend. Indeed, he was all but a dog himself. He came when he was called, he followed faithfully. While his master worked at his desk, Woira lay at his feet; and he had the complete freedom of the house, even to the kitchen. In temperament he was extraordinary. He was never known to be cross: not if he was denied something that he wanted; not if he was chased away from where he had no right to be; not if he was made to cease some ploy or game.

Even now, when Woira has been dead these two hundred years I grieve for him, and can scarcely bear to write his tale. He deserved so much better a fate. If only a Joy Adamson could have had him for his life!

The months passed, and Woira grew bigger and bigger. He remained gentle and harmless, as he had always been. But, say what you will, a nearly full-grown male lion must, as things are, raise apprehension. This came to a head when a child and Woira were playing together, rolling over and over on the ground. The boy was happy in this tumultuous, unusual game, and not in the least hurt. It was his watching mother who, perhaps reasonably enough, was terrified. M. Pelletan, knowing that Woira must grow bigger yet, and stronger with it; and fearing that one day, through no fault of the lion's other than his natural size and strength, just such a game might end in tragedy, decided that the time had come to put Woira under restraint.

Thus it was that he came to be sent to the King's menagerie at Versailles.

One must suppose that M. Pelletan minded parting with so biddable and fascinating a pet; on the other hand, he was probably a practical man and accepted as a matter of course that Woira could not stay with him for ever.

It is in accord with what we know of his kindly nature that he would not allow Woira and the dog that was still his constant companion to be separated. They made the journey together, and one may fairly safely presume that Woira had the run of the ship as much as the dog, as this was common practice with lion- or tiger-cub passengers which were accustomed to living with people.

The pair were disembarked at Le Havre; from there they went the rest of the way on foot, a distance of more than a hundred miles. The dog ran free, while Woira was led.

Arrived at Versailles, these two poor animals, accustomed all their short lives to complete freedom, were put into a small cage.

At first the noble, gentle Woira bore his captivity with the same resignation and good-humour with which he had borne any chidings in the house of M. Pelletan.

This could not last. How could he, who had been loved, petted and treated like a dog, understand why now he was closely confined and all his simple pleasures denied him? The irksomeness of his imprisonment was aggravated by physical pain. He was teething, and he had an ingrowing claw which had formed an abcess on the pad. Slowly, inevitably, shamefully, the generous kind nature was twisted to ill-temper. He, who had been so loved and so betrayed, now looked on everyone as his enemy. Except the little dog.

The years passed, bloody years of the Revolution.

It was because of the Revolution—as we are to see—that the remnant of the once great Versailles menagerie was moved in 1794 to the newly-founded Museum of Natural History in Paris; and thither Woira and the dog went. By this time Woira had been caged for six years. The dog was still his friend: the only bright spot in his tedious, curtailed life. They played together as ever. Only at mealtimes was their friendship slightly strained. They were fed at separate ends of the cage; and each respected the other's dish, knowing well that any other course would rouse fierce resentment and a quarrel.

On one occasion the keeper carelessly put Woira's share in the dog's corner, and gave Woira the much smaller ration meant for the dog. Poor Woira looked anxiously towards his meat (for the dog's meal was, on this occasion, bread), only to see his friend show his teeth snarlingly while he continued gulping down a "dinner such as he had never had in his life".

Not so very long after this the dog fell ill from lying with his back against a damp wall. Of this he died. Woira was inconsolable. He roared with grief, standing by the place from which the dog's dead body had been taken out of the cage.

When the roaring became less, it was because the desolate lion had lost interest in living. As the French so aptly puts it: he fell into *"une profonde tristesse"*; and every day his keepers could see he was getting weaker. He was a valuable animal, and they did not want to lose him. But let us give them credit, too, for having some heart. At all events, they decided that if he had another dog to keep him company he would regain his happiness and health. They took care to pick a dog as like as possible in appearance to the dead one. When this was found, they tentatively held it before the bars of Woira's cage.

Woira showed every sign of rage: roaring, lashing tail, claws outspread, the whole body tensed for springing. The keepers believed that he thought this was indeed his old friend one of them held in his arms, and that all the lion's wrath was directed at them for having stolen his dog from him.

They put the little animal in.

Woira killed it immediately. And never afterwards could he see a dog without going into nearly uncontrollable fury.

That at least is the ending that the eminent Gustav Loisel gives us; and his scholarship on wild beasts in captivity would be hard to beat. On the other hand, one cannot ignore a slightly different ending given by G. Toscan, the French naturalist: a man we will meet again in a later chapter, describing the lions in the Tower of London menagerie. This is quoted in a long note by the editor of the 1812 English edition of Buffon's *Natural History*. Toscan (writing of Woira, though he does not mention his name, only that of M. Pelletan) says:

"After his companion died, another dog was put into the lodge, towards which he was unjustly accused of cruelty. Terrified to find himself in company with a lion, the poor animal hid himself in the den, and made such a noise to get out of his confinement that the lion, willing to correct his ill-behaviour, gave him a blow with his paw which occasioned his death. A third dog was introduced in the room of the others, which he quietly suffered to live with him."

Whichever story is true, and I hope it is the second, Woira did to some extent get over his grievous loss. His health recovered; but he did not live for much more than another year, and his death in June 1796 was due to his not getting enough to eat in the general dearth that followed in the wake of the Revolution.

Evidently no lion is fooled by a substitute companion. At the Tower menagerie in London the same ruse was tried of giving another dog in place of an old friend that had died. The English keepers seem to have had less sense than their French counterparts. They offered this lion several live dogs, one after the other—one may presume with some days' interval—"but he tore them all in pieces pitilessly".

CHAPTER XIII

The Menagerie at Versailles

1

Since the French monarchs, as we have seen, had long kept collections of wild animals at most of their various residences, and to do so remained a necessary pomp for royalty, it is not in the least surprising to find that by 1662 Louis XIV, that magnificent sovereign who did everything on the grandest scale, was planning a superlative menagerie at his new palace at Versailles.

To Louis XIV must be given credit for the first really modern zoo: a zoological garden, as we understand the term. Before that at Versailles was built there had been no attempt to house the captive animals in one particular part of the demesne. They were scattered about, here and there. Now for the first time, at least in modern Europe, this was a *designed* menagerie, with the trees, plants, flowers entering into the design. The architect was the well-known Le Vau, who had been responsible for so much fine work on the Palace. The original garden, entirely walled in, took two years to complete; but it was added to and improved for several years afterwards. Incidentally, here as in many places in the Versailles pleasure gardens, one of Louis' favourite water-tricks was included: a grotto where an under-floor water system could be made to shoot up through tiny holes to soak the legs of the visitors!

Some of the cages sound modern in design: they had an upper apartment reached by a ladder.

This menagerie was stocked partly by presents from other crowned heads; but also—just as in the days of the Roman Empire—by animals sent back by the Governors of the French colonies and provinces. The ships of the two *Compagnies des Indes* (trading with India and America) were ordered to bring regular consignments of beautiful and rare birds from America,

Asia and Africa. Besides, once a year an animal-dealer, called Mosnier Gassion, was sent under the direct orders of Colbert (Louis' famous minister and financier) to Egypt and the Levant to bring back the less ferocious kinds of animals: such as deer, goats, ostriches.

By whatever means the animals were obtained, often the ships' masters objected to bringing back this difficult, space-taking cargo. Louis stood no nonsense of that sort. Through Colbert he issued orders to the respective consuls at the ports of embarkation to ensure that his animals were duly shipped.

Many of these creatures died on the long journeys home: journeys which averaged about two months, partly by land across their native continent and the rest by sea. They were disembarked either at Marseilles or Toulon, and at these ports kept for a time in quarantine. The end of the journey, as the beginning, was then completed on foot.

The Versailles menagerie (which, then, we may call the first modern zoological gardens, although that term had not yet been invented) was at first open to the general public: the only conditions being that the King was not in residence at Versailles, and that each visitor had a ticket.

This may sound reasonable to us. In fact, it was a totally novel idea to let the "common people" into the gardens of a royal residence to see the King's beasts. Before, if one was granted access, it was because one was either a personal friend of the monarch, or of noble blood or a courtier (the two being practically synonymous), a distinguished visitor; or, occasionally, an artist or scientist might be allowed in to draw or study the inmates.

A little later the condition of the King's not being in residence was waived, and the visitors needed only to get a ticket. There was even a Guide to the gardens, first published in 1674.

Even today Versailles is among the most spectacular and beautiful gardens of the world. Yet it takes great imagination and a good deal of knowledge to begin to see it as it was in the tremendous days of its glory under the *Roi Soleil* . . .

Louis was extremely interested in his menagerie. Every new specimen that arrived had its picture painted; and, as well, a miniature painted on vellum. Besides this collection of the King's personal pictures, many artists and sculptors came to Versailles to draw and to model. Again one must stress, keep on stressing, that many of the animals had never before been seen by the French people; and any pictures of them would be rare, possibly inaccurate, and in any case not readily available to the ordinary man.

One has only to recall the enthusiasm, the excitement, the crowds that pressed when, not so very many years ago, the giant panda, Chi-chi, first of her kind to be exhibited here, arrived at the London Zoo; and one may have a faint idea of what it meant for the public to see, not one, but several entirely new animals. No wonder they were said to give artists "a new source of inspiration".

Use was made too of the animals when they died. Through the dissection of their corpses the French *savants* were able to make great progress in the study of anatomy.

One exhibit which caused tremendous excitement was an elephant given to Louis in 1668 by the King of Portugal. It was the first elephant to have been seen in France for nearly eighty years; and the people flocked to gape at the rare, uncouth, amazing creature. Artists drew him; inquisitive persons measured his various dimensions, and zoologists sought to discover whether he indeed possessed the intelligence with which the ancient writers had credited his species.

How much they discovered on this score has not been recorded; but certainly this one was clever enough to unbuckle the tethering straps round his legs, even when the buckle was tied up with several knots. In summertime he was not in a cage: this was the way he was kept confined. So, undoing his buckles, one night he escaped. He did not go far, but during his walk he terrified all the other animals in the menagerie. This was simply by his bulk and his strangeness. He was a peaceable beast towards other creatures, tending to be nervous of them, particularly of little pigs!

To mankind he was less amiable. Many of the people who came to Versailles teased him; and it was soon noted that he remembered those who did. Everyone knows how elephants throw their trunks back and wait, large pink mouth exposed, for titbits to be thrown in. One of his tormentors, who had previously teased the animal by pretending to throw food and not doing so, tried his tricks a second time. The elephant was swift to be avenged. With a blow of his trunk he struck the man to the ground, then trod on him, breaking his leg. This was not yet enough, and he kneeled down, intending to pierce the man's stomach with his tusk, but—most fortunately for the intended victim—it went into the ground instead.

Another man who teased him was also accounted for. The elephant crushed him against a wall; and he was lucky to escape merely with severe bruising.

A further accident, though not so dire, happened when the elephant was being painted. The artist was doing him in the familiar pose of trunk curled back and open mouth. That he might keep the pose, the artist's servant had been ordered to keep on throwing into the exposed cavity bits of bread, apples and so on. Either the food supply ran out, or the man could not be bothered to go on with the game: anyway, like the fellow who had his leg broken, he made gestures of throwing with nothing in his hand.

The elephant's revenge was swift. He filled his trunk from a near-by source of water; and just while the artist was admiring his nearly-completed work, he whooshed out his entire trunkful, saturating both painter and painting!

This elephant's diet was fascinatingly different from the diet of a zoo elephant of today.

He appears to have had no hay. His daily fare was eighty pounds of bread and two buckets of a thick soup in which were steeped four or five pounds of bread. As a change from the latter, on alternate days he had two buckets of biscuits soaked in water. This is from the French account by Loisel: the English translation of Buffon turns the biscuits into two buckets of boiled rice. The idea of soup for an elephant is interesting enough; but one is left even more surprised on learning that every day he was given a gallon and a half of wine to drink. However, at that period it was common to supply certain animals with alcoholic liquors. And of course in France even the poorest people drank wine—of a sort.

The elephant got a good deal to eat besides from the many admiring visitors; and he also had a daily sheaf of corn. When he had eaten the grain, he would then use the remaining straw as a fly-whisk.

In summer he had a pleasant change of diet, as he was allowed to eat a lot of grass, breaking it off with his trunk.

In contrast, let us see the diet sheet for an adult elephant in the Bristol Zoo today. (After reading it no one is likely to contemplate keeping an elephant for a pet!) He receives daily 285 lbs of mangolds, 100 lbs of hay, a 4 lb loaf of bread, and also a handful of salt. From time to time he is also given vegetables (carrots, potatoes, cauliflowers, cabbage) and fruit.

The elephant at Versailles suffered a lot in the hot weather with chapping and splitting of his skin. (These keepers had evidently not heard of the cure of rubbing in fish-oil.) To stop the flies getting on his sores, the elephant would cover himself with dust, either by rolling in dust after bathing or, where he could, blowing the dust up with his trunk.

During the winter months he lived in a cage, and had, to keep him warm, a coal fire burning day and night.

We have given him the masculine pronoun all along—because that is what it was believed was appropriate. But when he died after thirteen years in the Versailles menagerie, it was discovered to the astonishment of all that in fact the elephant was a female!

The happy state of affairs of the public being free to come into this royal menagerie came to an end. And it was entirely the fault of the public themselves. As there are hooligans today, so there were then. They trampled the flower-beds, they damaged the statues, they overthrew the ornamental urns. Louis, naturally enough, objected to this, and he decided that he did not care to have such ill-mannered subjects about him when he walked in his own gardens. So, in the year 1699, he closed Versailles to the public and, as of old, only courtiers and their friends were allowed to come in.

It pleased Louis XIV that his nobles should follow the almost universal mode, and keep animals too. True, the nobles' menageries had, mostly, a utilitarian purpose, many of the inmates ending up in the kitchen. Not the monkeys, however, which it was fashionable to have disporting in one's house. Though perhaps we need hardly believe that these animals were as gifted as the claim made for a pet of a King of Spain: that he had taught her to play chess!

Madame de Montespan had a large aviary at St. Germain; and kept other creatures at the Château de Clagny. Of the latter Madame de Sevigny, in one of her many letters to her daughter, wrote waspishly that the King's mistress had *"pour plus de deux milles écus toutes les tourterelles les plus passionées, de toutes les truis les plus grasses, de toutes les vaches les plus pleines, de tous les moutons les plus frises, de tous les oiseaux les plus oisons".*

All who know anything of the life of Louis XIV know of his great fondness for his little grand-daughter-in-law, who was also his great-niece, the Duchess of Burgundy. She came to the French Court as a child; and was married when only thirteen years old. Before that, when she was barely twelve, the King had promised her that one day he would give her the menagerie. He implemented his promise when she was fourteen years old, and this coincided with his closing of the gardens to the public.

The young Dauphine and her ladies were to play in the menagerie much as Marie Antoinette and hers later played at Le Petit Trianon. She had a little château for her use, and could play the milkmaid in her own dairy. She was so young that she had many Arcadian summers; yet her life was very short, for she died at twenty-eight. Her death broke her old grandfather-in-law's heart. It is said to be the only truly great grief of his long life.

During the Duchess's time the menagerie had been greatly enlarged, and most of the animals from Vincennes were brought there.

Her son, Louis XV, succeeded to the Throne of France as a child of five: the same age that his illustrious great-grandfather, the *Roi Soleil,* had succeeded.

We have already told of Louis XV's brutality to his pet deer. He was no animal-lover, or even animal-admirer; and as he grew up so he lost interest in the menagerie. There is in fact no record of his ever having visited it. True, each new exhibit was shown to him in one of the vast salons of the Palace, but that was the end of his interest. During his reign the hitherto beautifully kept gardens and buildings fell into neglect. It was not the crowds now that destroyed them: simply, they were not tended. Where there had been trim lawns there were now fields of hay (grown to the profit of the gardener); and one may reasonably suppose there were weeds among the flowers, and straggling bushes once tightclipped . . .

His Majesty's interest was a little revived by the arrival, in 1748, of that rhinoceros which took Paris by storm—as recorded in an earlier chapter. It will be remembered that he wanted to buy it, but was not prepared to give the exorbitant price asked. He had to wait another twenty-two years before owning a rhinoceros. This was a young two-horned one, and the first male rhinoceros ever to be seen in Europe. This animal embarked at the Cape. He disliked intensely the pigs on board; and his particular companion was a goat which he allowed to stand beneath him while she helped herself to his hay from between his forelegs. She must have been either a very courageous or a very stupid goat!

In the following reign of Louis XVI the menagerie at Versailles became more and more neglected. Not only did this King too not go near it, but now the courtiers also kept away. It seems strange that Marie Antoinette, brought up at Schönbrunn with its fine menagerie, and so fond of her cows and model farm, had apparently no interest whatever in exotic beasts.

Since neither King nor Court any longer cared to wander there, the menagerie was again, after so many years, opened to the public. It remained in a neglected state, although some repairs were done, and some new exhibits were brought in. Among these was a two-year-old elephant who (except for the crossing of the Bosphorus) had walked every step of the way from Chandernagore on the eastern side of India. He was given much the same food as the elephant of nearly a hundred years earlier, including the wine. His diet also included—of all things! —a stew complete with onions, butter, salt and pepper.

He amused the visitors by drinking wine from bottles; and in return they gave him both brandy and tobacco. The account does not relate whether he became tipsy!

At least this elephant was not tormented like his predecessor by chapped, cracked skin. Every two or three days he was coated with fish-oil. One imagines he must have smelt rather unpleasant; but we are told of this treatment that he "loved it".

This elephant, ten years after his arrival, had a sad and unnecessary end. One night in 1782 he succeeded in breaking the chains by which he was tethered, and in the course of his wandering he fell into a basin or pond which had a great deal of filthy mud in it: "infected mire", the literal translation says. He appears to have been partly suffocated by this, and besides he had injured himself. In the morning he was, with great difficulty, moved; and the shifting of an immobile elephant must have been a tremendous problem. He never recovered from this accident, and died a few days afterwards.

Although the menagerie was quite abandoned by the Court and fashionable folk, yet during the last years of Louis XVI's tragic reign improvements were made, and much that had been neglected in the time of his grandfather, Louis XV, was now restored. In the 1780's there were several interesting exhibits: another elephant besides the one that had the accident, a female; a one-horned rhinoceros; a quagga (a beast now, alas! extinct); and, among other carnivores, the lion Woira.

Even as late as the year 1789 much was being done to tidy up and improve the menagerie; although during the next two stormy years economies were practised. These included doing away with all the aquatic birds, and most of the birds that were bred specifically for the royal table.

It was far too late for economies. The biting wind that is to sweep all before it is blowing now through Paris, through France, and the smell of blood is upon the air ...

2

Once the French Revolution had broken out, there could be no hope for the menagerie. When, three years later, the Republic was declared, it fell upon the worst days it had ever known, and many of the animals did not get enough to eat. It was considered —I suppose in the circumstances arguably—"shameful to feed beasts when men were starving". The trouble with that line of thought (and this is by no means the only time it has been used) is that though the animals go hungry it is exceedingly doubtful if any man actually benefits by a fuller stomach.

On the outbreak of the Revolution in 1789 a revolutionary club had been founded in the village of Versailles, which was later to spread to Paris, and its members to become well known as Jacobins.

In 1792 the Jacobins of Versailles, who had formed themselves into a group known as the *Société des Amis de la Convention,* made their decision. Through the streets of the village they came marching, flags flying, drums beating. To the great Palace (a prisoned King of France now, known only as Louis Capet), to the park, to the menagerie...

Here they routed out the ancient Director, a man called Laimant; and announced to him that all the creatures in his charge were made by God to be free; but they had been caged by tyrants. Now he, M. Laimant, must release them.

M. Laimant, who was in no position to argue, agreed. One may picture the frightened old man, white-haired, rubbing his hands, nodding his head, wanting to placate these wild, hungry-looking men who would think no more of spitting him on a pike than his cat would think of pouncing on a mouse... However, there was one consideration. Meekly he pointed out that some of the animals in his care were—as he quaintly put it—"inaccessible to gratitude", and, upon being given their freedom, their first act would most probably be to devour their liberators! Having said this, M. Laimant found the courage to say further that he would not take it upon himself to open the cages, but he would willingly hand over the keys.

It had not occurred to the members of the Society of the Friends of the Convention that gratitude might not be found in all imprisoned creatures given release; and the information gave them pause for thought. They held a consultation, and on a vote it was agreed that they should leave the ferocious beasts where they were. They then set about opening the cages of the others.

However well-intentioned such an action was, it showed this rabble to be men of no forethought or any knowledge of animals. How did they suppose that creatures, caged and fed many years, most of them from very different climates and terrains, could possibly fend for themselves? The did not think: like all political (and other) fanatics, having got an idea into their heads, no common sense could intrude to remove it. Tyrants—the wicked *aristos*—had caged these animals and birds: therefore they must be uncaged. As simple as that was their reasoning.

It turned out just as one would suppose. A few animals of the smaller sort did escape finally into the forest and survived. The majority were deliberately hunted and shot for the sake of their fur or skins. Others, who escaped this fate, died for lack of food.

Among the animals who made good use of their freedom were the Java rats. These multiplied so rapidly that, having taken refuge in and around the Palace, they did so much damage that eventually they endangered the foundations. Other châteaux in the neighbourhood suffered similarly.

It is an interesting sequel to this story that fifty years afterwards descendants of the survivors of creatures released from the menagerie were still being found in the forest of Versailles. The then Inspector of Forests made a count of "quite a number of very interesting and exotic" animals caught or killed.

When the Friends of the Convention did their work there could not have been many very fierce beasts in the menagerie (unless they overcame their scruples and shot them). At any rate the record reports that all that was left consisted of one "superb" rhinoceros, the quagga, a couple of deer and, besides a few birds, Woira and his dog. The only understandable captives are the rhino and poor Woira—whose diet, incidentally, in these hard times had changed from beef to horse. Why they should have feared the quagga and these two particular deer must remain a mystery. Perhaps the animals simply refused to leave.

The rhinoceros was to meet its end in almost exactly the same way as the elephant twelve years earlier. It fell into an artificial basin and was badly cut. The wound turned gangrenous, and although the rhinoceros—rather surprisingly, considering the times—received expert veterinary treatment, it grew worse.

Meanwhile much discussion had been going on as to what was to be done with the few animals that remained of the Versailles menagerie. It was decided—this was in April 1794—that they should be sent to Paris and put in the *Jardin des Plantes*. The rhinoceros was too ill to move, and he died the following month, still at Versailles.

For some time afterwards the site of the menagerie was used as a sort of experimental farm for the breeding of sheep and cattle.

There were of course many other menageries in France. The fate of Chantilly we have already seen. Nearly all the great aristocrats had, if not menageries, deer-parks, and parks where llamas, alpacas and vicuna ran. All were taken over by the revolutionaries. Some were opened to the public; in others the animals were slaughtered.

As the blood-filled years passed, so the feeling grew that collections of wild animals were symbolic of the bad old days when gentlemen still strutted in their splendid gardens. *All* wild animals, even those belonging to the humble *forains,* or travelling showmen, began to be seen as representative of depraved aristocratic taste.* Anyway, the creatures—so far as menageries and parks went—were taking up valuable land. Worse than this, they needed food which was better given to men. So—nearly all were killed.

In Paris alone the thin thread of menagerie history remained unbroken.

It was in 1793, before Woira and his fellow-captives were taken to Paris, that the police of the new *régime* began confiscating in the name of the State all the wild animals belonging to the travelling showmen of Paris. They took, too, the bulls kept for baiting and fighting. These probably had a more merciful use in being killed outright and used for food.

The owners of the confiscated wild beasts, no aristocrats, objected strongly. They had had to pay large sums for such animals as lions and bears, and now they had no means of livelihood.

These animals, belonging, after all, to good citizens, were not killed. The Convention had seized the Royal Garden in Paris, and it now announced it was to be a Museum of Natural History. In other words, a zoo: a people's zoo. This was a part of the *Jardin des Plantes,* and at this time the two names were often used for what was virtually the same place. The showmen's confiscated animals were to form the nucleus of this zoo.

When the first batch arrived, twenty-six of them, mostly of ferocious species, there was nothing ready. Not sufficient accommodation, and if there had been, no money with which to pay for their upkeep or for any keepers.

What a situation! The animals were a gift from the Paris Commune: a gift that, in the circumstances, the newly-appointed Professors of the Museum and those of the *Jardin des Plantes* were most unwilling to accept. Discussion raged. Some said forthrightly that the unsolicited gift should be refused and that the Commune had no right to force it upon them. Others sug-

* We can see a little of the same notion in our own generation in the violent opposition to blood-sports. Hunting (wrongly as to fact) is seen, even if subconsciously, as a symbol of wealth and arrogance.

gested the arrivals should be killed, and the Museum of Natural History could then exhibit them stuffed instead of living. This, requiring neither food bills nor keepers' wages, must have seemed an attractive solution. But it was then pointed out that there were as yet, so new was the Museum, no facilities for dissecting, mounting skeletons or preparing hides.

In the end, somehow they managed. The living animals were accepted, and some kind of accomodation was found for all of them.

Their indignant late owners who through the arguments had been, as it were, clamouring at the doors of the Museum and the *Jardin des Plantes*, were now not only paid some compensation for the loss of their beasts, but some of them were given employment as keepers.

That was not the end of it. For the next six months confiscated animals continued to arrive, and presumably more and more accommodation had to be built. Then it was the turn of the remnant of the Versailles menagerie to be moved here; and that, for the time being, completed the Museum of Natural History.

This zoo did not flourish. Food was scarce, and the State unwilling to provide much money for the well-being of mere animals; so, by the following year many of the inmates had died.

That this living Museum was not, through mismanagement and stinginess, completely wiped out was thanks to a newly-appointed Director in 1795, a man called Mordant Delaunay. Under his care the animals again began to thrive; and the stock was increased by creatures brought back to Paris as trophies by the conquering armies of the Republic.

Yet the problem of food remained, in such troublous times, an obstinate difficulty. Four years later the animals were again dying of starvation.

It was Napoleon who saved the Museum, and brought menageries into favour again.

Rebuilding began in earnest in 1802. Napoleon, then First Consul, had recently inaugurated the *Croix de la Légion d'Honneur*, and in deference to this the house for the big grass-eating animals was built to a design incorporating the shape of the Cross, with the outdoor runs between the five arms. It was described as "cold and ill-lit".

Building went on for the next twenty-five years.

CHAPTER XIV

A Tale of Two Elephants

Among the lesser upheavals caused by the French Revolution was one as far away from Paris as the *Groote Loo* menagerie in Holland, which, until the Republican army arrived, had belonged to the Prince of Orange.

The Princes of Orange owned two menageries: one, the *Groote Loo*, near Apeldoorn; the other, the *Kleine Loo*, within one mile of the Hague.

Here, in the year 1784, two elephants, male and female, had arrived from Ceylon, aged between eighteen months and two years. They were very tame and friendly, and became at once great favourites. Both the *Loos* were country houses, and the elephants were allowed to wander freely in the Palace of the *Kleine Loo*, even walking up and down the staircase. They attended meals, and "all were fascinated by the dexterity of their trunks". Consequently, they scooped up many a titbit. Often the pair were walked into the Hague, and led about in the streets. They are described as being "the delight of the Court and the town".

After a year of such spoiling—and it must have been a regretful decision to make—the elephants were sent to the *Groote Loo* (or Great Loo as opposed to Small Loo), as there would be much more room for them there.

At this time the *Groote Loo* menagerie—or *Het Loo*, as it was usually simply called—had the reputation of being the "most interesting in Europe to a naturalist", because of the number of rare animals kept there.

Here the elephants, whose names were Hans and Parki, stayed for a happy ten years. Their keeper, at least towards the end of this time, was an Englishman, a Mr. Thompson: evidently settled in Holland, as we are told he was "of English origin". Mr.

Thompson taught his charges tricks: quite simple ones like taking a piece of bread from off the tops of their heads; or, at command, they would turn themselves right around so that a visitor could see them at every angle. He would also put his hand into their open mouths.

Hans and Parki were very obedient, and seldom needed to be chided. However, if they ignored orders or misbehaved in any way the punishment was to be chained up by one foot on a heavy twelve-foot chain. On these occasions "the culprit submitted with a contrite air", and would take hold of the chain with his (or her) trunk and shake it.

These elephants' most attractive attribute was the depth of their devotion to each other.

A M. André Thouin, a member of the *Institut de France* and of the Museum of Natural History, and therefore presumably a man not in the least given to sentimentality, wrote of these two elephants that they "loved each other with a true love, one might even say with a human love when one saw, in the park where they walked in liberty, the male seizing the high branches of trees with his trunk so that the female might more easily eat the leaves."

This idyllic life, wandering free, only chained occasionally as a deserved punishment, ended abruptly in 1795 when the French overran Holland. It was the same story as at Versailles, at Chantilly, and any other menageries in the path of the revolution. There was no longer enough food for the animals, and neglect, starvation and misery overtook *Het Loo*.

We may be very proud of our fellow-countryman, Thompson. He was told that Hans and Parki were to be killed, because there was not enough for them to eat. Thompson at once declared that henceforth they would be his entire responsibility, and at his charge. On those conditions they were reprieved. Thompson must have had some savings he was ready to sacrifice for his beloved elephants; for not only would it have been very difficult to find sufficient fodder for them, but scarcity would mean an exorbitant price asked. But Thompson has not yet finished his good work.

A certain Frenchman who had some kind of official position under the Republic, took it upon himself to treat the menagerie as his private property. Some of the animals he removed—probably to sell for their meat or hides—and, almost worse, he would go out armed with a pistol and shoot the most brilliantly-plumaged birds, the golden pheasants, Chinese ducks and other species.

The last straw for Thompson was the day this horrible man shot a splendid moose: an animal that "was the admiration of naturalists and of the curious". If the moose was shot today, what was to prevent this fiend coming tomorrow—or any day soon—and shooting Hans or Parki?

Thompson in his indignation found the courage to go to General Dejean, who was in command of the French troops, and told him what was happening. That it was not an easy thing to do is shown by the wording of the account, which says that Thompson "dared" to tell the General.

Fortunately this officer was sympathetic. But the man who was doing the damage was not a soldier, so he could not be simply ordered to stop pillaging the menagerie. The General, however, had great power as the Commander in occupied enemy territory, and he gave orders that the menagerie was not to be molested; what was more, he sent a detachment of soldiers strong enough to ensure that his orders were obeyed.

Very soon afterwards the uncertain confusion that always follows in the wake of war was straightened out by a Convention between the States of Holland and the French Republic. Under the terms of this *Het Loo* passed officially into the hands of the French. This was in February 1795.

It was now decided that the inmates of the menagerie should be sent to Paris, to the *Jardin des Plantes,* to which the few remaining Versailles animals had already been moved.

Transport was a difficult matter. Not then convenient motor-trailers or trains: the horse-power of living horseflesh only. Consequently, the removal was not immediate. Much preparation had to be made. Indeed, a full year was to pass before nearly all the menagerie departed, conveyed on ten ammunition wag-gons, each drawn by four horses. This journey took from February 1796 until the following August.

Left behind at *Het Loo* were only some deer, sheep, birds —and Hans and Parki.

It was not intended that these two should remain behind. Their travelling accommodation was still building. That the elephants should walk from Holland to Paris does not at any time appear to have been considered.

Thompson, as soon as the political situation had been clarified, had shrewdly insisted on being paid all the arrears he was owed: not only his wages, but also what he had spent on the upkeep of the elephants. Nor would he accept the paper assignats issued by the French Republic: he must be paid in good internationally-recognized money. A true-born Englishman, Thompson!

By June, four months after the first contingent had left, the wagons for Hans and Parki were ready: two vast ones specially made, each strong enough to support a very heavy cage and an elephant weighing some tons.

In point of fact Hans and Parki are not going to reach Paris for nearly two years...

The journey was scheduled to start on the twentieth of the month. Hans was led into the new "half-dark" travelling cage. Accustomed to liberty and the companionship of Parki, he did not like it at all. He attacked the bars with both trunk and tusks, and it was soon realized that his great strength had been underestimated. He tore out the bars, unluckily breaking one of his tusks while doing so; then, trumpeting with triumph, he rejoined Parki, awaiting her own boarding.

The cage was ruined. There could be no more talk of setting off that day. Nor for very many days. Four months passed before a new and stronger cage was ready.

Led towards this, Hans remembered his last adventure, and was rightly suspicious. He refused to enter. They got him in at last by means of an ingenious trick.

Hans was very intelligent, and all the men engaged in the difficult manoeuvre of boxing him knew that he would be suspicious of any grown person who tried to bait him. So a little boy—and no doubt there were several standing round watching—was given his orders.

Hans was placed facing away from the cage, and was tethered behind by one leg so that he could not come any further forward. The child then threw potatoes just behind Hans' front feet. To reach them he had to step backwards. More were thrown, and the chain correspondingly shortened, as he stepped back again; and so on, until the poor beast had unwittingly walked backwards into his cage. There must have been anxiety as to whether Parki too was going to be difficult. She proved amenable, and was easily led into her cage.

So this unwieldy *cortège* started. An impressive sight it must have been, with sixteen horses straining at one of the huge "chariots", and fourteen at the other, with the two uneasy elephants, securely chained, aloft.

But Hans and Parki were not yet destined to leave *Het Loo*. They travelled a mile or so to the gate of the great park; and, going through this, in some way the enormous wagon carrying Hans got caught up in part of the iron railings. Details of the damage are not given, but it would seem that one of the wheels had been smashed, as there was "considerable breakage", and all the efforts of the sixteen horses were unable to budge the vehicle.

Carpenters had to be sent for, and repairs began. For four days the men worked in an effort to make the wagon fit to continue on its long journey. It could not be done. It was only possible to patch it up sufficiently to hobble home again.

"Discouraged" (as we are told), all returned to the menagerie, Hans and Parki to take up residence again in their old permanent apartments.

It is touching to read of their pleasure. They trumpeted, both deeply and shrilly. "It was a song of joy; tears streamed abandonedly from their eyes, caused by pleasure and tenderness." They caressed each other unceasingly with their trunks.

This, though they had not contributed to it, was a singular victory for the elephants. It was now seen that the wagons, in spite of having been rebuilt once, were not even yet strong enough to undertake the long journey to Paris.

Hans and Parki remained undisturbed for nearly a year, during which time new and stouter vehicles were being made.

Finally, on the 25th September 1797, they set off again. This time it was determined they should reach journey's end. The wagons, Hans' still pulled by sixteen horses and Parki's by fourteen, were accompanied by a veritable army: a hundred horsemen and a detachment of artillery.

Thus they successfully got upon their way. As soon as it was possible, the wagons were transferred to boats; and so, both by river and canal, they reached Rotterdam. Here they stayed some days. Then taking boat to Dordrecht, they crossed the sea inlet down to Bergen-op-Zoom. This proved a rough crossing, but the elephants' keepers (Thompson of course was in command) were impressed by the intelligence both Hans and Parki showed in bracing themselves against the considerable movements of the ship. They arrived at Bergen three weeks after leaving *Het Loo*. A night was spent at Antwerp, then they proceeded, still by water, down the River Escaut, to Ghent.

Here the journey was broken for ten days. The elephants were not allowed to leave their cages at any time on the whole trip. No doubt it was foreseen that it might be impossible to get Hans inside again; nor were they taking any chances with Parki. At Ghent it was Parki who fretted most. In her unavailing efforts to get loose she too broke one of her tusks; so now both had, to the same extent, spoiled themselves.

From Ghent they went down the river to Cambrai. From here their way lay by road to La Fère, before they could again take to water and come via the Oise and the Seine to Paris. At Cambrai it was learned that the road of their proposed route was in exceedingly bad condition, full of holes and ruts. Autumn was well advanced by now, and with the prospect of snow and ice it was decided that the only wise course was to winter at Cambrai, and continue the journey in the spring.

The time was well spent. A commandant of engineers and his men carefully examined the wagons, and all the parts weakened by jolting, knocks and the strain of travel were repaired.

When this work had been completed, the commandant proposed to mend the road to La Fère. He tried to employ the Cambrai townspeople to help him and his men but, for whatever reason, they refused to do so. Without sufficient labour slow progress was made, and all he was able to do was to have the worst of the holes filled in.

During all these months poor Hans and Parki remained in their cages, so placed that they could not see each other. Presumably it was thought that if they did their frustration would be so great that they would injure themselves even if they could not break out of their prisons.

The long winter over, they went—as it is described—"from jolt to jolt" down the rough road to La Fère, which lies north east of Paris. From here, by water, they came to the capital, tying up at the *Porte des Invalides* on the 23rd March 1798. The entire journey, by land and water, was 160 kilometres and had taken six months.

That same evening Hans and Parki were taken to the *Jardin*

des Plantes. Fine apartments had been prepared for them: certainly the authorities had had plenty of time in which to get them ready! But, probably because it was already late, they were left in their travelling cages till the morning.

Hans was let out first. He walked into his new house with caution, deeply suspicious. He examined it from top to bottom, feeling with his trunk up and down the walls everywhere that he could reach. He even tried to turn the big screws which held the timbers together. Thompson gave him food, and, reassured, he quietly began to eat.

Then Parki's cage was opened. She was so delighted to be released that she gave a cry of pleasure. In her excitement and interest she did not immediately see Hans in the adjoining and connecting compartment. The keeper called Hans by name. He turned. And this is how an eye-witness describes the meeting of these two lovers who had not seen each other since they had left *Het Loo*:

"At once the two animals ran to each other, giving cries and whistlings so loud and piercing that the whole building was shaken. The joy of the female appeared the greater; she expressed her feelings above all by the rapid flapping of her ears, which she moved as a bird moves its wings. She passed her trunk over the body of the male with the greatest tenderness and the greatest voluptuousness. She concerned herself particularly with his ear, which she held a long time; often, too, after her trunk had wandered all over the male's body she returned it amorously to her own mouth."

Here in Paris they could not have as much freedom as they had known at *Het Loo,* but they were very popular with the public: so popular that there had to be an armed guard always by their cage to prevent the spectators from feeding them. (This was surprisingly advanced thinking: it is only very recently that most zoos have found it wiser to forbid indiscriminate feeding by the public; and at this time it must have been practically unheard-of.)

Hans and Parki had a sensible and less exotic diet than earlier elephants. Neither soup nor wine, but just the same as they had had in Holland: hay, potatoes, carrots and bread.

Parki, at least, resented the—to her—officious guard who prevented her admirers from giving her titbits. On one occasion she doused him full in the face with water from her trunk. Naturally enough the crowd laughed and, while the man was recovering from his discomfiture, someone else tried to hand the elephant a morsel. The man quickly stepped forward, flourishing his gun threateningly. To his amazement, and the unconcealed delight of the spectators, Parki's trunk whipped out again and seized the gun from his hands; she then twirled it in the air like a corkscrew. Having obtained both laughter and applause for this feat, Parki politely returned the weapon to its owner!

It is well known, and has long been understood, that animals are affected by music. Sometimes—as in certain dogs—only to the extent that they will howl. Cows are said to give their milk more readily when soft music is played by the byre.

Whether to test this theory of animal appreciation, or simply because Hans and Parki were such an attraction, it was arranged that sixteen musicians from the *Conservatoire* should give a concert before the elephants' cage. The Professors of the Museum of Natural History and other "privileged people" were invited to attend. It was no classical concert. Popular music of the day was played: such tunes as *"Ça ira"*, *"O ma Tendre Musette"*, *"Charmante Gabrielle"*.

Hans and Parki listened attentively, and to everyone's surprise showed varying emotions according to the gaiety or the sadness of the airs.

In this connection it is interesting to find that a similar experiment was tried comparatively recently in the New York Zoo. This is what happened.

"While the band played a *paso doble* the elephant shed enormous tears; two lions, busy devouring their meal, left their food and stood there listening; the wolves and tigers seemed to be enchanted; the bears, stags and gazelles all started to dance.

"A Strauss waltz, which was played immediately afterwards, nearly sent them all to sleep; Chopin's *Funeral March* brought forth a chorus of mournful wails; a jig, on the other hand, calmed them down again.

"After the concert the bears, the stags and the gazelles all went on dancing, while the lions and tigers began to howl, as they moved up and down their cages." *

* From *Il Nostro Tempo* 26th March 1950; quoted by Elena Quarelli in *Socrates and the Animals (Socrate e le Bestie.)*

Hans and Parki, for elephants, were short-lived. They were not above fifteen to sixteen years old when they arrived in Paris. Not quite four years later Hans fell ill with attacks of fever. Whatever his illness may have been the poor creature had very great pain with it, so much that in his anguish he broke one of the bars of his cage. His sufferings were cruel, but we will not dwell on them. Enough to say that one night, after he had been ill a little over a fortnight, he was very restless and kept on bellowing. Towards four in the morning his cries changed in character, becoming sharp and shrill. Parki had been brought in to try to comfort him. She was greatly moved by his agonies, and tried to lift him up, while tears poured copiously from her eyes, and all the time shé uttered cries such as no one had ever heard from her before.

All was of no avail. About six o'clock in the morning Hans died. It was right and fitting that Parki should be with her beloved at the end ...

As her lonely days passed, Parki fretted so greatly that all were in deep concern for her health, and feared that she too would die. The professors conferred together, examined her, deliberated. Obviously, she was dying; not of any illness of the flesh, but solely of grief.

They hoped that a companion might go some way towards assuaging her loss.

But an elephant is not as easily obtainable as going out to buy a puppy, or even a pony. In the confusion of France at that time it was even more difficult than usual to know where to obtain one. In fact, an elephant could not be found. The Professors made do with a camel. We do not hear that Parki was unkind to the camel; but she certainly did not accept him. She grew thinner and thinner. If another elephant could not be found undoubtedly she would die.

At last, in July 1803, eighteen months after Hans' death, a male was bought at Rouen Fair. He cost 16,000 francs.

Unfortunately it is not recorded how Parki received him. But she remained faithful to Hans. This one, they said, arrived too late to save her. Parki continued to decline, and died a year later.

Surely these two, Hans and Parki, though "mere" elephants, rank among the great lovers ...

CHAPTER XV

In Austria

Although many noblemen had for long kept some animals, if only the living representatives of those depicted in their coats-of-arms, the earliest menagerie in what is now Austria (and it is convenient to call it thus, if not strictly accurate) was founded by Maximilian II of the Holy Roman Empire at Ebersdorf, near Vienna, in 1552. It began with his hunting-leopards and an elephant that he brought back from Spain. This was not the first elephant to have been seen in these parts. The previous year a travelling showman had been walking the country with one. At least one inn, overwhelmed by the honour of temporarily housing such an animal in its stables, changed its name forthwith to *Zum Elephanten*. This hostelry, not far from Innsbruck, retained its name into the present century.

One scarcely associates a pelican with being an interesting and companionable pet; but Maximilian had one which went everywhere with him, and not in a cage either, but flying free. It even accompanied him when he was in the field with his troops: an original sign, certainly, for picking out the Commander-in-Chief! This pelican lived to be twenty-four years old.

As well as Ebersdorf, Maximilian founded another menagerie, at Neugebäu. This survived longer than Ebersdorf, which ceased to exist at the beginning of the 17th century.

During the reign of the Emperor, Leopold I, that is, during the latter half of the 17th century, a terrible adventure befell a young girl in the menagerie at Neugebäu. Here the lions were so tame that the keeper's daughter, who assisted her father in his duties, used to go into the dens every day to clean them, and to feed the lions.

In course of time this young woman became betrothed, and

her marriage-day came round. Of course at that time people did not go away on honeymoons; and, other than the ceremony and feastings, for poorer people there was no other break in their routine.

Thus it happened that, still in her bridal dress, she went as usual to feed the lions. She entered first a den, or, rather, the pit outside the den where, in this case, a single lion lived.

One must not of course imagine her in a long white dress and flowing veil. Probably her dress was quite simple. The point is that it was different from the clothes the lions were accustomed to seeing.

Now, animals are very sensitive to a change of apparel. This can be observed even in domestic creatures. The horse or ass, used to seeing the owner in slacks and shirt, may well shy away with snorts of disapproval on seeing instead, say, a patterned silk dress and a straw hat.

However that may be, this lion at Neugebäu became alarmed at the change in his young keeper's appearance; either because he did not recognize her, or he thought she had become an enemy.

On the other hand, M. Loisel, whose opinion I very greatly respect, suggests that the lion may have been jealous, for jealousy, he says, is "very developed" in lions.

The lion did not attack her. He simply lay down in front of the door leading out of the pit, and would not allow her to pass him.

He had more than the patience of a cat at a mouse-hole. This unhappy bride was thus imprisoned in the lion's cage for several days. One can only suppose that the agitated watchers, including the frantic husband, did not dare to set one of their number to shooting the beast for fear of wounding it; when indeed the girl's life would certainly have been forfeited. Food and water must have been lowered to her, and perhaps warmer clothing. Fitful sleep she would have, sharing a cage with an irritated lion.

Day after day, night after night, they must have hoped the lion would leave his guarding: but always he was there.

At last they tried a desperate remedy. A length of rope was let down: not, as is one's immediate conjecture, for the girl to climb up (when she would almost certainly have been clawed down by the lion), but for the far more difficult purpose of attempting to haul up the lion. At length, somehow, this intrepid young woman managed to get one end of the rope round the beast's body, and some kind of a knot made. "Profiting by a moment of inattention in the lion", those above began to pull. They were not—could not be—quick enough. The lion sprang aside, onto the poor bride, and tore her to pieces...

The menagerie at Neugebäu had a stormy history. In one of the many Hungarian revolts against Habsburg rule, it was, in 1704, sacked, and all the inmates killed. The pillagers skinned such beasts as were suitable, and took their pelts for furs.

Some years later it was re-established by the Emperor Charles VI, but now housing only carnivores. Its history after this was not long. It survived till the time of Maria Theresa, though diminishing in numbers. In 1781 the last animals were sent to Schönbrunn.

To go back. Maximilian's successor, Rudolph II, owned the first cassowary to be seen in Europe; or, indeed, probably anywhere outside its native Australia. It was the Dutch who brought it back. First, it was exhibited at Amsterdam and then bought by the Elector of Cologne, and given as a present to Rudolph.

It is hard for us, living in a world where communication is so rapid and the entire geography so well known, to have the slightest conception of the sheer excitement and wonder attending the discovery of a whole vast continent—though how vast no one could yet have guessed. Here was an entirely new species of bird. What other fascinating, fantastic animals would be discovered? All natural historians must have been on tiptoe with expectation. There is nothing comparable today—not even a moon-landing, for the moon is barren.

In the event the naturalists were not to be disappointed. As is now common knowledge, many species on that great continent have no counterpart anywhere else in the world.

Of the many menageries that rose and vanished in the next two or three centuries, the most notable was that of Belvedere, belonging to Prince Eugene of Savoy. He began collecting his animals in 1716, and by the time he had finished Belvedere was probably the most beautiful zoo of its time.

Although the Prince heartily hated Louis XIV, he admired what he was doing at Versailles, and his own plans owed much to the menagerie there. It was a most attractive layout; and could be said to be so too from the inmates' point of view (insofar as captivity can in any way be attractive). The animals' quarters were built in a big semi-circle round a fountain, with a wide promenade between fountain and cages. It is necessary to see the menagerie layout like half of an enormous cake, and the seven wedge-shaped enclosures like seven slices of cake, though not coming so far as to a point: the fountain would be the point. At the rim of the cake (furthest from the promenade) are the seven dens, each with access to its run or slice.

These open enclosures each had some turf and a pool; and were divided one from the other by a wall, and on each side of each wall was planted a row of trees. Very formal, and very much in the 18th century style, and most graceful. Where the people looked in from the promenade, they were separated from the animals by handsome and elaborate wrought-iron railings, with wrought-iron gates into each enclosure.

This lovely menagerie did not long outlast its maker. After the Prince's death the Emperor, Charles VI, bought the Château of Belvedere. He sent all the fierce animals to the menagerie at Neugebäu, keeping at Belvedere only those described as "peaceable". As the years went by, the numbers even of these gradually diminished; and less than forty years after Prince Eugene had created his zoo at Belvedere, it was no more; the remaining inmates having been sent away to the newly-opened menagerie at Schönbrunn, near the Vienna woods. The only exceptions to this exodus were a golden eagle, which had been a favourite of Eugene's, and a white-headed vulture—perhaps kept for company for the eagle. However that may be, the vulture, who was known to be alive in 1706, lived through the century and finally died, still at Belvedere, in 1824. A record, surely, for vulture longevity!

The menagerie at Schönbrunn was built in 1752 by the Emperor Francis I; and was designed on the same lines as that at Belvedere, only larger, with thirteen "slices of cake" instead of seven. It increased rapidly, and in less than ten years there were from six to seven hundred animals and birds. The birds included such domestic species as pigeons and hens; and indeed the feathered inmates accounted for a third of the whole menagerie.

As has been mentioned, it was here that Marie Antoinette

grew up. She is so famous as the guillotined Queen of France that it is sometimes forgotten she was daughter of the Emperor Francis I and Maria Theresa. It may well be that it was the memory of her childhood at Schönbrunn that made her want to have a little play farm at Le Petit Trianon. In the fine summer weather, she and her family used to lunch every day in an ornamental octagonal pavilion in the middle of the menagerie.

In those days it was not open to the public. That was to come later, in the next reign, that of Joseph II, brother of Marie Antoinette. He increased the menagerie; but the bad days were drawing near.

What eventually destroyed Schönbrunn (before it rose again) was what destroyed so much in Europe: the rise of Napoleon.

On his way to Austerlitz with his army in 1805 he had passed it; and on returning after his great victory, he came that way again.

The Superintendent, knowing what had happened to so many menageries: Versailles, Chantilly, *Het Loo,* to say nothing of innumerable small private ones, craved the Emperor that he would spare Schönbrunn. Napoleon, whatever his faults, appears to have been fond of animals. At any rate he is said to have "freely played with" the gazelles he kept at St. Cloud. He reassured the man, and took the menagerie "under his particular protection".

In spite of this the *Intendant-Général* of the defeated Emperor of Austria's household sent to the Museum of Natural History in Paris a list of everything in the Schönbrunn menagerie, and also in the neighbouring botanical garden, asking if there was anything the Museum would like to have. Why he thus betrayed the Superintendent I do not know. But this quisling was successful, and eventually all that was left in the once fine menagerie were four kangaroos and a pair of Lapland ponies. Then these, too, were taken away to be exhibited as spoils of war of the *Grande Armée.*

Later, this zoo was reopened; and it is interesting to find that it was here, in 1852, that giraffes bred for the first time in Europe.

CHAPTER XVI

Human Menageries

It has already been told how Montezuma kept a collection of freaks and deformed persons as an appendage to his collection of mammals, birds and reptiles. Freaks, though, hardly come into the category of a human menagerie: deformed people even less so. It is only very recently (in this century) that the showing of freaks has, on humanitarian grounds, fallen out of favour. Before, they were a part of every fair; and one does not have to be very old to remember seeing the Fat Lady, the Giant, or a Tom Thumb who could sit in a top-hat. Our grandparents' generation saw worse: such as malformed twins, so that one body had two heads and a double number of limbs.

No, the real human menageries were perfectly logical, and the desire for them understandable. In the beginning of mankind's history, and for a long time afterwards, travel far from home was not an accepted concept. Everyone was too busy wresting a bare living. Then, as we progressed, and began to move about, naturally it was of staggering interest to discover that all human beings did not look like one's neighbours. Even today many find it difficult not to be jolted by the fact that somebody's skin is quite a different shade from their own! So it is not in the least surprising to find that great men who were able to obtain specimens of different races liked to exhibit them alongside their exotic animals. What *is* surprising is how hardly this idea died: one attempt happening a bare hundred years ago.

René, Count of Anjou, whom we have already met as the owner of the biggest menagerie to be found in France in the 15th century, and who liked all curiosities, kept foreign human beings too: Turks, Negroes and what in the record are lumped together as "barbarians". There is no need to suppose that these men were kept in cages—even Montezuma did not cage his freaks. Probably they simply had their apartments, and had to put up with visitors intruding on them whenever René wished it. And no doubt they had to do some work as well.

A hundred years later Cardinal Hippolyte of Medici kept what one might call a real human zoo. His collection, (inevitably referred to as a "troupe of barbarians") consisted of more than twenty different races, including Moors, Turks, Negroes, Indians, Tartars; and for all his specimens he had endeavoured to get the handsomest representatives that could be found.

Such collections of men were by no means uncommon at this time, and later. They were to be found at the Courts of Savoy, Turin and Angers.

Negroes were exhibited for the first time at Lisbon in the 15th century. One may well imagine that they caused no less interest than the redskins from North America, brought back by Jacques Cartier in the next century after his second journey to Canada, and put on show in St. Malo, his native town.

At Amsterdam in the 18th century two freaks were actually kept right in the *Blaauw-Jan* menagerie, alongside the animals. These were a giant, 8 feet 9 inches tall, and a twenty-six-year-old dwarf who was only 29 inches high.

The most ambitious attempt to found a general and geographical zoo never got off the ground. Its would-be progenitor, a French architect called Verniquet, said—and with truth!—that if his ideas were carried out they would "add more, if that were possible, to the glory of Bonaparte's Consulship". So this dates it between 1799, when Napoleon became Consul and 1804 when he assumend the title of Emperor.

This zoo, which would cover a great deal of ground, was to be divided into four parts, each representing respectively Europe, Africa, America and Asia. The necessary mountains were to be made, the plains, the rivers, the ponds. In each section would be seen the indigenous animals and plants of that continent; and to care for them would be the indigenous population, each wearing his native dress and living in the kind of house or dwelling he had left behind him. M. Verniquet does not seem to have considered how the unfortunate man from the equatorial belt of Africa would manage in a French winter with only a line of beads about his middle; or indeed how the Eskimo was to keep his igloo frozen!

In any case his idea had a cool reception. Certainly the State could not afford to execute so grandiose a scheme; and besides, the Directors of the *Jardin des Plantes*—who were destined to run it—had no wish at all to take it on.

As late as 1873 we find in Sweden a "living zoological and ethnical museum". This, to be sure, consisted of Swedes only. Dr. Hazelius, who created it, began by moving from different provinces of Sweden the old wooden buildings: churches, farms, houses, mills. These being assembled in their varying villages, he brought in the peasants, who had not only to wear their national dress, but must keep up their local customs, songs, dances, games. The people established, then the appropriate plants and trees were planted. Last of all the animals belonging to the different regions were introduced.

Such an artificial "zoo" could not of course last. It took eighteen years to found and, as far as I can learn, had ceased to exist ten years later. The motive behind so extraordinary a venture was not to make a spectacle, not to make money; but a praiseworthy effort (lost before it was well begun) to stop the "fatal slide which seems to lead all people into the hopeless, irreversible uniformity of bourgeois civilizations".

The last recorded "human zoo" (excluding simply freaks, which are still, in parts of the world, on show) was that of the Great Barnum (the American, Phineas Taylor Barnum) towards the end of the last century. Alongside his menagerie of animals, he had one which did include many freaks, albinos and deformed persons, but as well Zulus and other "savages".

Since, in the nature of things, the supply of freaks could not keep up with the demand they were often faked. A dead freak, preserved, was easier still to impose upon the public. Although pygmies certainly are not freaks, as long ago as the 13th century, this was being done—according to Marco Polo—with the dried bodies of alleged pygmies.

He was writing of a practice in Sumatra, although he called it India. So much of the old-time world, ranging from the Americas to the East Indies, was described as India that it tends to be confusing.

"I also wish you to know that the pygmies that some travellers assert they bring from India, are a great lie and cheat, for I may tell you that these creatures, whom they call men, are manufactured in this island; and I will tell you how. You must know that in this island there is a kind of very small monkey, with a face like a man's. They take these monkeys and, by means of a certain ointment, remove all their hairs except round their genitals; then they stick into their chins certain long hairs to look like a beard. Then they dry them. As the skin dries, the holes into which the hairs have been stuck, close, so that the hairs look as if they had grown there naturally. Further, as their feet, hands and certain other members are not quite the same as those of a man, they pull and shape them with their hands, and so make them similar to those of a man. Then they put these beasts out to dry, and shape them, daubing them with camphor and other things, until they look as if they had been men."

CHAPTER XVII

The Tower Menagerie

Through the centuries, in England as everywhere, the terrible combats, the atrocious baitings, went on, and on, and on... An entertainment gloated over from the lowest in the land to the highest.

King James I (and VI of Scotland) was an insatiable attendant at the gory shows staged in the Tower of London. He particularly liked watching dogs, perhaps three of them, pitted against a lion or a bear. If they were victorious it would be a wonder if they did not have to face another ... and another.

During that famous winter of 1683-4, when the Thames was frozen solid for weeks and there were incessant fairs and junketings, bulls had to be baited upon the ice; and unfortunate tethered cocks to suffer the stones hurled at them in the despicable sport of cock-throwing.

We cannot, and should not, forget these unceasing cruelties, but we will not dwell on them further.

Unlike the Royal Parks, the Tower menagerie had always been open to the public; and for centuries "to see the lions" was a favourite outing, particularly on a Sunday, hardly less for the gentry than for the common man. The entrance fee was at first a penny (though it was to rise to sixpence) or, if prefered, one might in lieu of money bring in a live dog or cat to give as food to the inmates. No doubt this form of payment was very popular with the other visitors. There was not much squeamishness in our forefathers. (Are we any better today? It was no worse a death—almost certainly a quicker and more merciful one—than abandoning a dog on a motorway.) Another grisly note on food. When the surgeons had finished dissecting bodies, the remains were taken to the menagerie, and helped to swell the meat ration...

For long it was an old April Fool's Day joke that on that day one could see the Tower lions being bathed!

Lions were always the chief attraction. In Elizabeth I's day all were named after Kings and Queens. It was considered an ill omen—rightly, as it turned out—that the lioness Elizabeth should have died while her namesake was ill: for from this illness Queen Elizabeth did not recover.

It was at the very end of the 17th century that the first hyena was shown in England. The poster advertising him stated that "he hath such great strength that he breaks the biggest of ox-bones, and eats them". Of a later hyena the *Guide* to the Tower menagerie remarks: these animals have "two joints more in each foreleg than any other animal". They might have added the information from one of the bestiaries that "it can only turn round in one piece as its spine is rigid"!

In the reign of Anne the number of lions had risen from six a century earlier to eleven; and there were, besides, two other great cats (the record not being sure whether these were leopards or tigers), two wild cats, a jackal and three eagles.

A newcomer in 1739 was probably the most exciting addition to the Tower menagerie since Queen Elizabeth I's elephant, given to her by Henri IV of France nearly two centuries earlier. This was a rhinoceros from Bengal. The cost of it, with carriage, was nearly £1,000—an enormous sum in those days.

The rhinoceros's diet, as well as "great quantities of hay and grass which it chiefly preferred", was seven lbs of rice mixed with three lbs of sugar, all this being divided into three separate meals. It also drank "great quantities" of water.

In 1754 the Tower menagerie consisted of only two lions; and of other animals: "two bears, three tigers, one leopard, two tigers *(sic)* "two Egyptian night-walkers" (and I don't venture to suggest what those may have been!), "two monkeys, one racoon, one jackal, one tiger-cat" (probably a serval), "an ostrich, several eagles and an owl."

One racoon kept in the menagerie was very fond of oysters; and he was given them too. It is a safe bet no modern racoon enjoys this luxury! In those days, of course, they were common as winkles and food for poor folk.

The first official description of the Tower animals that I have come across is dated 1774. A second edition came out in 1789, and it is from this one that the quotation below comes. The author was modest and published his work anonymously under the unwieldy title of *An Historical Description of the Tower of London and its Curiosities*. Naturally, the animals only take up a very small part of this thin volume.

The visitor to the menagerie is instructed "... when you have entered the outer-gate, and passed what is called the spurguard, you will see the keeper's house just before you, which you will know by the figure of a lion being placed against the wall: and over the door where you are to enter is another figure of a lion; and there you ring, and for 6d. each person you will presently gain admittance, and be shewn such a noble collection of wild animals as is no where else to be seen in Great Britain."

One entered first into the half-moon-shaped courtyard described in Chapter V, where were still kept the great cats, mostly lions, but also leopards and tigers.

One lioness, called Fanny, had come from Algiers in the care of a Moor; and she was so tame that she used to be led about by "a string". When the Moor returned to his own country, poor Fanny was so disconsolate that she beat herself against the bars, and pined till the keepers feared she would die. In an effort to console her she was given—just as was Woira—a dog for company; and, although in Fanny's case it was a man she moaned for and not a lost animal companion, the remedy proved entirely successful. Fanny loved the dog so much that he quite got the upper hand of her: to the extent that he would not let her eat until he had had his own fill!

Lion-breeding in captivity was never highly successful until the last century when the Dublin Zoo gained an international reputation in this field. Lion cubs are hard to rear, and, in the days before scientific feeding, succumbed easily, particularly at teething time. The lions in the Tower did breed, but few cubs survived. At the time the *Guide* was written one of the lionesses had had five litters; but only one of all these had lived to become as big as its mother, then it too had died.

On the other hand, longevity was not unknown. On the authority of Oliver Goldsmith and also of the editor of the 1812 English translation of Buffon, we learn that "the great lion called Pompey" died in the Tower in 1760 at the incredible age of "above seventy years". The latter also tells of another, "which was brought from the River Gambia [and] has since died ... aged sixty-three".

To return to our *Guide*. Attention is drawn to Sophia, a beautiful leopardess from the East Indies, so amiable that "the sailors used to make a pillow of her when on board, she being both tame and loose on the voyage."

Besides, there was "an extraordinary curiosity, a Black Leopard called Jack being spotted, though black; but the spots are blacker than his coat, and is the first ever seen in the world". This animal had been sent by Warren Hastings as a gift to King George III.

Of the two tigers, described as Royal Tigers, one was from Madras, the other from Bengal. The former "the largest ever brought to Europe, and very savage, not liking to be disturbed when shown." The other was "reckoned to be the most beautiful tiger in all England". (The competition, one feels, could not have been keen!)

After seeing the great cats in the half-moon courtyard, the visitor proceeded into another large yard, known as the Second Range. Here were kept the smaller, less exotic animals, the eagles and other birds.

There was no ostrich in the Tower in 1789, but one had recently died: a fact which reminds our author of an ostrich in Amsterdam which, soon after its presentation, died as the result of "swallowing iron nails, which the populace threw to it, upon a presumption that it could digest them like other food; but, the ostrich being opened, about 80 nails were found entire in its stomach".

Unfortunate ostriches belonging to travelling showmen quite often died from eating the pennies the crowds gave them. It was generally believed that ostriches could digest anything.

Another contemporary account of the lions at the Tower was written by a visiting French naturalist, author, and librarian to the Paris Museum of Natural History, G. Toscan. This would be about ten years later.

"The first that we were shown was called Princess Didon, she was then in all the vigour of her youth, aged six years and perfectly beautiful. The second is called Jenny. We were told she is about forty years old. It was the oldest lion that they had ever seen in the Tower,* although it is more than five hundred years that they have maintained these creatures. She had been the mother of nine cubs, all sons of a lion called Marco, who is no longer alive. These nine died at an early age with the exception of Nero, now dead two years and who had lived ten, and of Nancy, who had lived double. It was only with great difficulty that they were able to save these last two cubs, because there are no animals more difficult to rear, because of convulsions which they get when teething. They keep them during the first year in a warm room, and feed them on milk. They were as gentle as lambs, but their natural savagery soon developed with their strenght, and at three years old they were as fierce as those from abroad.

"The third lion we saw is called Helen, aged seven years; she is still a maiden, but is all ready to wed the first supplicant who shall present himself."

As the years passed the Tower menagerie began to be neglected, and the number of animals diminished until, in 1822, there were only an elephant, a grizzly bear and some birds. This bear was, and remained for many years, the only one of its kind to be seen in captivity in Europe.

George IV, perhaps sorry to learn that so ancient and interesting a place of entertainment was in danger of dying out, now took a hand. He appointed a man called Alfred Cops to be in charge, and arranged that the menagerie should be greatly improved and added to. So successful was this scheme and Cops' administration that seven years later there were on show sixty species of mammals and birds, not counting the monkeys; and snakes besides. Some of the exhibits appear to have been the private property of Alfred Cops, and he made some profit for himself by showing them.

Once again there were great cats at the Tower. A lion and lioness arrived within a year of Cops' appointment. These, while

* This discounts both Goldsmith and Buffon's editor. However, I am informed by an expert that such life spans for lions are not possible. In captivity they do not live more than twenty to twenty-two years.

they were still cubs, roamed as free as dogs among the visitors. In their native land their mother had been shot and they had been fostered by a goat, and then sent home as a present to the King.

There was also a tiger brought up from a cub who, until he arrived at the Tower had never tasted raw meat, but had "had his food boiled", and he was very fond of soup! It was thought that this diet was the reason he was so good-tempered. Once he was in the Tower no doubt he had his raw meat the same as the lions. Their ration, fed once a day, was eight or nine lbs of beef, excluding bone weight.

This is interesting, as it approximates so closely to the amount of meat fed to the lions in Bristol Zoo today: eight to ten lbs, with the bone perhaps twenty lbs. What the Tower lions lacked was a vitamin supplement meal put on the meat, as is now given. In the wild state any carnivore gets a certain amount of grass from the stomach of his newly-killed prey; and this vitamin meal gives him the equivalent good of this. Without it, cubs can be born deformed.

Earlier we saw that Woira's diet, through pressure of the French Revolution, was changed from beef to horseflesh. In Bristol Zoo at least, and probably in all other British zoos, during the last twenty years horseflesh has largely taken the place of cattle meat; and this is chiefly due to the great number of riding schools which have sprung up in this time, with the consequent casting of aged and unfit horses. It has been found that the great cats prefer to eat horse; and if they have had it for several years, they refuse any other flesh.

To give cubs the natural food they would get in the wild, that is vegetable matter, fur etc., their mincemeat contains minced whole mice and day-old chicks, and often wheat is minced in too.

The question of diet is a fascinating one. Who today would give a tiger soup, or an elephant either, let alone wine and beer, as was done in our forefathers' time?

One of the most extraordinary accounts of animal feeding—if we may digress for a moment to domestic animals and to a far time and place—comes from Marco Polo. Writing of Eshier (more properly, Esh-Shihr), a province of south Arabia, he declares "their cattle, namely their sheep, oxen, camels, and ponies, eat fish. That is their food, for the whole region and district is without grass, being the driest place in the world ... The fishes that these animals eat are very small, and are taken in the months of March, April and May in such enormous quantities that it is truly a wonder. I will add that they dry them and store them, dealing them out to their cattle in the course of the year. But the animals will eat them alive too, just as they are taken from the water."

He also tells that at Malabar, "They feed their horses on meat cooked with rice, and on many other cooked foods."

Back in London and the 19th century, we may remember that many animals easily acquire a liking for alcohol. The elephant in Cops' time was still being given wine and spirits. The account adds that an intake of alcohol will often make elephants obedient when all other means have failed. (Presumably he becomes too drunk to mind!) This particular elephant drank (*not* all in wine) thirty or forty gallons of fluid a day; and he ate a hundredweight and a half to two hundredweight of solid food.

In those days there were not the same safety barriers between the public and the cages as are to be found in modern zoos. So looking at the exhibits, if one was careless, could be reasonably hazardous. The leopardess, for instance, was in the habit of putting out a powerful paw and seizing from the ladies their parasols, their muffs, even their hats; all of which, it need hardly be said, were immediately in tatters. Mr. Cops is on record as remarking that the leopardess had had as many of these trophies as there are days in the year.

These animals were probably fairly generally teased and poked at. To most of our forbears there was simply nothing wrong in tormenting a caged animal. There is a very revealing remark written in 1782 about a caged lion belonging to the Duchess of Hamilton. As a matter of course the guests who had been brought to look at him teased the beast with sticks "to make him fly at us".

There is a happier anecdote about this lion. A sergeant who had had the care of him on the sea journey from Gibraltar three years earlier, came to see him.

When the sergeant arrived the lion was eating his dinner. He watched him and called out:

"Nero, poor Nero! Don't you know me?"

At once the lion left his meat and came to the bars, showing every sign of delight.

One can surely conclude that that day at least he was not teased.

Zebras, as is well known, are not very biddable to bit and bridle. The Burchell's zebra in the Tower, however, allowed a boy to ride her; and she would follow her keeper loose all about the precincts of the menagerie, never leaving him except to go to the refreshment booth where those in charge usually could not resist giving her a draught of ale, a beverage she was "particularly fond of".

Of course there have been many efforts to break such showy equines to harness, but success has certainly been limited. Yet there seems no really sound reason why a zebra should be so much less easy to subdue than a horse or an ass. No wonder it was a persistent dream! How dashing, how eye-catching to drive a pair, or a tandem, of these dazzling animals!

In Portugal, about forty years before Cops took over the management of the Tower menagerie, Princess Marie had zebras specially brought over from the Congo for the purpose of breaking them in. This certainly seems a forlorn hope; unless she had bred foals from them, and perhaps in a generation or two got them domesticated. On the contrary, she seems to have been a lady of great optimism. A little covered carriage was made, and splendid harness prepared, the equipage to be for the use of the royal children, that they might, behind these exotic animals, drive about their mother's park. As might have been foreseen, the zerbras would not co-operate! They refused "to allow-themselves to be harnessed to it". That was the end of that experiment, and the harness was sent, possibly as a reminder to future generations of the futility of such an attempt, to the Arsenal Museum. As for the zebras, they became the nucleus of the menagerie at Queluz: one destined to last but a short time, as it ended after the Royal Family had to flee their country on the invasion of the French in 1807.

Josephine, at Malmaison, was more successful with zebras. She kept a small zoo there, and a zebra was the "ordinary mount of her children."

A later effort was made to domesticate zebras. They were

crossed with mares, a hybrid that seems to have been first seriously bred in Brazil around 1892. Twenty years later these crosses were to be seen in harness in Paris, so the experiment must have been reasonably successful.

We have wandered rather far from the Tower of London and the riding-zebra there.

It was William IV who finally and for ever closed the Tower menagerie, after an unbroken near six hundred years of history. London Zoo was then forming, and he gave all the Tower stock to it, as well as the considerable number of wild animals kept at Windsor.

It is convenient here to mention the travelling menageries which, while in a small way they had existed since at least the Middle Ages (if as no more than a man with a couple of monkeys and a bear), now in the 19th century came to their zenith. Usually they were combined with a fair and a circus, and names such as William Cooke and Barnum were as well known as, in this century, say Bertram Mills or Chipperfield—a family which has been in the animal-training business a very long time.

These spectacles were immensely popular; and it is merciful for the animals that, in this country at least, they have largely fallen out of favour. Or, where they have not, public opinion demands better conditions for the beasts. Woeful indeed were the narrow cages and the constant jolting journeys by wagon.

As well as performing in a circus ring wild animals were, at this time, used on the stage in a way which would make the hair of modern theatre-goers stand on end. For instance, in Paris, in 1831, a famous animal-trainer called Martin (he who planned to found the *Zoorama*) put on a play in three acts and seven scenes called *The Lions of Mysore*. It must have been one of the most breathtaking entertainments staged since the Roman extravagances. In one scene two "immense" boa-constrictors wrapped themselves around the bodies of two children. A little later a band of Indians was attacked by a pair of lions; and one may safely presume this was done realistically enough. As a finale there took place on stage a tiger hunt, the quarry visible, and the hunters mounted on an elephant.

Another trainer—whose family is famous to this day—was Hagenbeck.

Carl Hagenbeck was the son of a Hamburg fishmonger. As a youngster he used to go to the harbour to collect the fish for his father's shop. One day the men had brought in a seal, and this he bought "very cheap". He spent his spare time teaching it to do tricks; and then showed it in public for a few pfennigs. The turn was so popular that he acquired five more seals; and by now was far more interested in training animals than in fishmongery. Gradually he enlarged his exhibition; and later, so successful were his methods, he was also training animals for established circuses. Eventually, buying the land in 1903, Hagenbeck was to found the Hamburg Zoo.

CHAPTER XVIII

From Exeter 'Change to London Zoo

Before looking at the very early days of the London Zoo, direct child of the Tower menagerie, mention must be made of another—in its day—very famous show of wild animals. This was at Exeter 'Change in the Strand. The building was on the site of Exeter House, home of the famous Lord Burleigh, of Queen Elizabeth I's reign.

Exeter 'Change had shops on the ground floor, with accommodation above, and this had originally been occupied by a business known as the Exeter Exchange Company of Undertakers. A very flourishing concern it was, and long after the undertakers had departed the name of Exeter 'Change (always thus shortened) remained. The building was demolished in 1830.

Here, from approximately 1773, was one of the most unusual menageries: unusual, because all the exhibits were in the upper rooms above the shops, possibly housed on three floors, but certainly on two. Nor were they only small animals. Among the earliest exhibits was a rhinoceros. It would be interesting to know how it was persuaded to mount the stairs. Or, for that matter, its successor thirty years later.

This menagerie was first opened by a man called Pidcock. Down at the docks he had noticed that when wild animals were disembarked, crowds always gathered to stare at them; so he decided that here was a money-making proposition.

When Mr. Pidcock had got his animals housed, he put at the door a man dressed up as a Yeoman of the Guard to do the "barking", and persuade the people to come in. Among the animals to be seen were lions, tigers, elephants and monkeys. (One cannot help wondering whether some at least of the plurals were an exaggeration!)

We know from J. T. Smith, the author of that once popular book of reminiscenses, *Book for a Rainy Day,* that an elephant arrived about the year 1785. Mr. Smith was walking late at night with a friend, and being by Temple Bar they were astonished to see an elephant being coaxed to pass through it. This elephant, they discovered, was making his way from Tower Wharf to Exeter 'Change. Two men were on either side of him with ropes, and several others went behind with "tall poles".

Later on, Mr. Smith, now with another friend, a baronet, had, as he says, "the honour... of partaking of a pot of Barclay's Entire with this same elephant." This was when the two men were looking at the animals in the 'Change menagerie. The keeper had announced that if a shilling was given to the elephant it would nod a health and drink a pot of porter. "The elephant had no sooner taken the shilling, which he did in the mildest manner from the palm of Sir James's hand, than he gave it to the keeper, and eagerly watched his return with the beer. The elephant then, after placing his proboscis to the top of the tankard, drew up nearly the whole of the then good beverage. The keeper observed, 'You will hardly believe, gentlemen, but the little he has left is quite warm': upon this we were tempted to taste it, and it really was so."

After Pidcock the exhibitor at Exeter 'Change was Polito, and he was followed by the much better known Edward Cross.

As one walked down the Strand the menagerie was very well advertised. The building jutted out onto the street, and on the side wall in large letters were painted the words *Royal Menagerie* (though it had no connection with His Majesty), and underneath were painted pictures of some of the beasts and birds to be seen inside.

The entrance was flush with the Strand, and over the portal were more pictures and, of course, the name again, with the added information: *Dealer in Foreign Birds and Beasts.* So it would seem that it was a market for wild animals as well as a menagerie.

Admission was half-a-crown: a stiff entrance fee for the times.

Inside, the walls of the animals' cages were painted with scenes to resemble the kind of land from which each had come. This was imaginative on the part of Mr. Cross, but it must have been a more than usually miserable captivity enclosed in a building, with no access to the open air. Incidentally, the roaring of the lions and tigers in this strange upstairs zoo frequently terrified horses passing in the Strand below.

In 1809 an elephant arrived. This one must have had accommodation at street level, because he came and went nightly to Covent Garden, being one of the performers in *Blue Beard*. He was called Chunee, and was a great favourite with the actor, Edmund Kean, who used to give him loaves of bread; in return Chunee would caress Mr. Kean with his trunk.

Edmund Kean was fond of animals. He owned a puma, which followed him about like a dog, and which he often brought into his drawing-room, sometimes to the consternation of his visitors.

The unfortunate Chunee was to come to a terrible end.

For seventeen years he was at Exeter 'Change, and then he became "ungovernable... through the return of an annual paroxysm". The decision was taken that he would have to be killed. A squad of soldiers was commissioned to do this. Alas! they knew nothing about killing elephants; nor, evidently, did Chunee's owner take the trouble to inquire if they did. The soldiers had no shot heavy enough to pierce effectively the thick hide, and the horrifying number of one hundred and fifty-two bullets were fired before the great beast, weighing five tons, and standing eleven feet, fell.

Valued alive at £1,000, he did not fetch much when dead. The hide, weighing seventeen cwt, was sold to a tanner for £50; and the skeleton was bought by the Royal College of Surgeons for £100. It was put in their museum in Lincoln's Inn Fields.

Later it was to be said that the greatness of Exeter 'Change departed with Chunee.

Chunee has been confused by subsequent writers with the elephant which J. T. Smith and his friend watched drinking a pot of beer. That elephant was, as we have seen, in the menagerie some twenty years earlier; and, besides, J. T. Smith specifically says that later it was "disposed of" for one thousand guineas.

The most surprising and unusual of Edward Cross's exhibits was the white tiger to be seen in Exeter 'Change in the year 1820.

This lovely ghostlike beast, with its shadowed stripes and

topaz eyes, is no albino and breeds true, as has been well proved at Bristol Zoo. There the only white tigers in Europe are to be seen.

Two years after Chunee's death, that is in 1828, the entire menagerie from Exeter 'Change was moved to the King's Mews, on the site of the present National Gallery.

In the meantime the Zoological Society of London was in process of forming our now famous London Zoo. Gifts of wild animals were arriving and, as the Society's premises were not yet ready, the Keepers of both the Tower Menagerie and of Exeter 'Change were asked to house them.

Later Edward Cross offered his whole collection to the new Society, together with the suggestion that he should become manager of their Zoo. Both offers were declined.

After this failure Cross took on the management of a rival zoo being planned by the Surrey Zoological and Botanical Society on the south bank of the Thames. It is interesting to find that this was landscaped by Richard Forrest, who laid out the gardens at Clifton for the Bristol Zoo, (or, to give it its present full title, the Bristol, Clifton and West of England Zoological Society) which was first opened to the public in 1836.

However, for some reason the Surrey zoo did not flourish, and what became of the animals I have not discovered. It is certainly likely that in the end they went to the London Zoo.

Here is no place to go into the history of the Zoo in Regent's Park. Only one or two comments on its early days are relevant.

The very first keeper employed was one James Cops, obviously of the same family as Alfred Cops who had so successfully administered the Tower menagerie. He was appointed in June 1827, and his wages were one guinea a week.

Even the London Zoo does not appear to have been very flourishing in its earliest days. At any rate it was reported in a Victorian newspaper that after it had been open "little more than two years", there was in it neither lion, tiger, elephant, rhinoceros nor hyena.

But to come to its prosperous Victorian days.

One of the early attractions for the public—who love to sup on horrors great and small—was the feeding of the snakes on live prey. As P. Chalmers Mitchell, who was Superintendent of the Zoo in the early years of this century, puts it: This practice "passed with most persons as a plain necessity and with many as an engaging spectacle".

However, there were people who protested, Charles Dickens among them. It did not stop for many, many years; but public opinion had been thus much roused that by 1858 it was no longer advertized in the Zoo *Guide*.

By the time Mr. Chalmers Mitchell was appointed Superintendent the feeding of live prey had officially discontinued in public. But only in public. Out of sight of the visitors the reptiles were still thus fed; and a tip to the keeper could always ensure one might see a live rabbit, or even a goat, being taken. This was now completely stopped, the only exceptions being if, for some particular reason, it was absolutely necessary to feed with a living creature.

Mr. Chalmers Mitchell's findings on the attitude of the prey to its reptilian predator may afford comfort to the squeamish. He writes:

"I had noticed with special interest... that no one of the living victims ever showed any signs of a specific dread of the snakes. Rats and mice, rabbits, pigeons, chickens and even goats were much less disturbed when they were put in the cage than when a human being tried to take hold of them. They were all quite indifferent to the presence of the snakes, and even when one of the reptiles approached them directly, they avoided it just as they would avoid a stick thrust at them. The only creatures that I heard making a noise, even when actually caught, were frogs."

Mr. Chalmers Mitchell was obviously fascinated by the legendary power of snakes to terrify by their mere presence. He made experiments with harmless snakes among almost every animal and bird in the zoo.

For instance, he put a snake in with a young orang-utan that had been taken very early from its mother. His intention was to discover whether the apes' natural fear of reptiles was instinctive or acquired. He learned that it was the latter. "The orang-utan was not in the least alarmed, but took the snake as a new and attractive toy, playing with it, allowing it to coil over him, and treating it with such friendly roughness that I had to remove it."

All older apes and monkeys were frightened of the snakes. With a few exceptions everything else "would come down to the front of the cage, peck enquiringly at or try to smell the swaying head, more ready to see if it were good to eat than afraid of being eaten."

Among the more interesting arrivals of last century was the hippopotamus in 1850. This, from the White Nile, was believed to be the first specimen to have been seen alive in Europe since the days of the great animal spectacles in Imperial Rome.

More interesting still (with hindsight) was the quagga, that fascinating equine, looking to be half-zebra, half-horse which —and we should never be done lamenting this—we can never see again. It was hunted to extinction, and it was one of the last representatives of its race which came to London Zoo from Cape Colony in 1859, the second (and last) to be shown there.

There are people who still hope that in some remote part of Africa the quagga will be found again. Because of the terrain they like, this is very improbable; and, as far as is known, the last quagga in the world died at Amsterdam Zoo in 1883. That was a unique animal for eight years, as the only other known quagga had died in Berlin Zoo in 1875.

It is rather surprising to learn that the first zebra was in the Gardens as late as 1864.

The first gorilla came in 1869, only to die seven months later.

As for the aurochs, which was claimed to arrive in 1847, this was a misnomer for the European bison, or wisent. The true aurochs, a species of wild European bull, had been extinct for nearly a hundred and fifty years.

According to Loisel, the last authenticated specimen was seen in the park of the Count of Königsberg, in Poland, in 1669.

A pair of Père David's deer (or mi-lu) were presented to the Zoo by Sir Rutherford Alcock, our Ambassador in Peking, four years after they were discovered in 1865.

They were already semi-domesticated then. About three miles south of Peking there was a huge sandy plain entirely surrounded by a high wall, and this place for centuries had harboured herds of deer. They were never hunted; and if anyone did get past the Tartar guards and kill one, that man was put to death.

Here was a true park of conservation, rare indeed in the old world.

Father Armand David no doubt asked many questions about this imperial deer-park. One thing he learned was that no European had ever entered it. So he showed great courage and curiosity rather than caution when, on a spring day in 1865, he climbed up onto the wall and was rewarded by seeing a herd of more than a hundred of this unfamiliar deer, which at first he took for elk.

As far as is known, they have never been seen anywhere wild. All the known specimens today—and of course there are many in England, notably at Woburn Abbey—stem from the herd in the park near Peking.

It was as well that in the next few years several specimens were expatriated, for if they had not been this deer would now be extinct. In 1894 the River Huang-ho flooded to such an extent that the wall of the hunting park was breached, and the deer escaped into the open. Many were killed for food by the peasants who saw their rice-crops ruined or in peril. Those which avoided this fate were practically wiped out six years later in the Boxer Rebellion. Only two are said to have survived: these must have been kept in captivity if it is true that the last one did not die until 1921.

Since then a few Père David's deer have been sent back to China.

Nothing is known of the origins of these deer. They are more like deer native to the continent of America than deer from Europe or Asia. Indeed, they differ from any of the latter two by having no brow-tines on the antlers.

One of the most fascinating zoological events was the discovery of a large, hitherto unheard-of mammal, so astonishingly late as in the year 1902. The okapi, whose existence was not so much as suspected, was found by the explorer Sir Harry Johnston, his curiosity roused by the sight of an unidentifiable hide on a native drum. At first this animal was called the Johnston's zebra. Sir Harry was awarded the second gold medal ever given by the Zoological Society of London. The first was, by comparison, merely a token one given in 1877 to the Prince of Wales (later Edward VII) in "acknowledgement of his many valuable donations to the zoo and other favours".

What a strange and lovely creature the okapi is, with its soft, so velvety-looking rich-brown fur, striped hind legs, and its gentle, inquiring expression. No zebra, but half-deer, half-giraffe.

Are there any other such discoveries to be made; or have we truly rifled this marvellous treasure-chest into which we have been born? Perhaps in the white and silent heights of the Himalayas there will be captured at last the huge, mysterious, manlike creature known for long to the people of the foothills as the yeti. Or shall a name and a classification one day be given to that baffling and controversial monster that is said to trouble the waters of Loch Ness and of Loch Mora?

That will indeed be an exciting day.

CHAPTER XIX

A Word about Windsor

It was George II's son, the Duke of Cumberland (he who bore the unenviable nickname of the Butcher of Culloden) who introduced wild animals into the park at Windsor. This was about the year 1764 when he commissioned the East India Company to send him some beasts, his choice of species, alas! apparently being governed by their suitability to provide entertainment for himself and his friends by fighting each other, or, as a matter of course, for chasing or being chased.

Among the animals was a brace of big cats, unequivocally described as tigers in the account about to be related. These were in fact almost certainly cheetahs; and that was the opinion of the menagerie historian, Gustav Loisel.

One of these cats, tiger or cheetah, was put into a canvas-walled arena in the park, and a stag was put in with him: for the amusement of the Duke and his friends.

"The tiger at once sprang at it, meaning to seize it by the flank; but so well did the stag defend itself with its horns that the tiger was forced to retreat. Again the tiger sprang, and tried to seize the stag by the neck. He was repulsed with the same vigour; at last, at the third attack the stag, with a blow from his horns, threw the tiger quite a distance, and then went after him."

By this time the big cat had had enough, and he managed to escape under the canvas out into the forest. He hid himself among the trees and—what must have been to his pleasant surprise—found himself surrounded by a herd of hinds. He then instantly killed one, and was busy feasting on it when the two Indians in charge of him found him. They were prepared for his capture, and threw a large cloth over his head, then put a chain upon him. Obviously, this was a fairly tame animal, as the men allowed him to finish his meal before they muzzled him and led him away.

The Duke was so pleased with the valiant stag that he had a silver collar made for it, on which was engraved the story of its victory. When the collar had been put on, the stag was let loose again in Windsor Park. One may perhaps safely presume that this distinction rendered it immune from the attentions of, at least, legitimate hunters.

The strong argument for the stag's opponent having been, not a tiger but a cheetah rests not only on the latter being a far more common hunting animal; but also (though admittedly inconclusively) on the fact that it is known that in the following year George III, nephew of the Duke of Cumberland, owned at least one hunting cheetah, and this animal also was in the care of two Indians.

This cheetah of 1765 has become world famous; for it is the one that Stubbs painted: a painting which in March 1970 fetched the record price for a Stubbs, changing hands at Sotheby's for £220,000.

The animal was given to George III by Sir George Pigot, Governor of Madras, and the two Indians sent with it. It was intended by its donor to be hunted and it was no more reprehensible to use it in this way than if it had been a trained hound.

It was arranged that it should be let loose in Windsor Great Park to chase a stag. Notice was given of the event, and a great crowd gathered.

The cheetah was duly loosed in the presence of a stag. It looked round bewildered, unnerved by the presence of the crowd. Not for all the persuasions of the Indians—who must have been hot with shame for their charge—would it move. It refused to budge. There was no hunt.

This is the subject of Stubbs' picture: the still cheetah, the Indians gesticulating and persuading in vain. An interesting point remains. Stubbs also painted the stag, standing quite close and looking, it seems, with interest rather than terror, at the spotted cat. A later owner of the picture, Sir Robert Pigot, presumptuously decided that no stag would stand thus calmly so close to a cheetah; and, in 1822, he had the stag over-painted: a fact which certainly must shock all admirers of Stubbs! Only in 1960 was the picture restored to its original condition.

Now, what I find particularly interesting is, that in the newspaper photograph of this picture (not as clear as one would wish) the stag appears to have a collar about its neck. If this is indeed so, then obviously this is the famous stag which had recently successfully overcome another cheetah (or, even more formidable, a tiger), and therefore was sufficiently fearless to stand near by. If this is so, George Stubbs had made no error.

Though deer were to remain in Windsor Forest, all the wild animals were, with the Tower collection, presented by George IV to the newly-formed London Zoo.

Approximately one hundred and fifty years have passed; and again lions and other beasts are roaring and roaming in Windsor Park in the recently opened "Safari" attraction . . .

CHAPTER XX

The New Morality

It will be remembered that very long ago, when the bestiaries were being written, and even before that, the study of the animal kingdom was inextricably bound up with the glory of God, and therefore with moral behaviour.

This idea, rather different in form, came to life again in the 19th century in both Düsseldorf and Helsingfors—or, as it is now more generally known, Helsinki.

The Directors of these zoos each had the old, highminded idea that their Gardens could be used for "moral education". For, of course, the young men were being tiresome as, in every century, the young tend to be!

It is difficult to see what the worthy directors of Düsseldorf Zoo hoped to achieve. They could hardly have expected that mere contemplation of the beauty and wonder of animals would turn hooligans into law-abiding, responsible, citizens. At any rate they were not having much success with their plan until, very early in the present century, a wealthy philanthropist came to the rescue. He thoroughly approved of what the Zoo authorities had been trying to do; and he spent his money in making the place more interesting and attractive, in the hopes that the local young men would prefer to come there rather than waste their time and money in taverns. This benefactor was a Herr Scheidt, and he did so much for the Zoo that it was given his name.

Still, it seems doubtful if any zoo could hope to compete in the long run against the beer-halls.

The menagerie at Helsinki was actually built and owned by the Helsinki Temperance Society: a body which with great cunning had managed to get the monopoly of the profits of all alcoholic drinks sold in the town. They paid their shareholders 5%, which was nowhere near the true profit, and the remainder of the money was spent in fighting alcoholism. A truly Alice in Wonderland situation! The zoo, of course—as at Düsseldorf—was designed to be a counter-attraction to the taverns.

That issue may be in doubt; but it was—and is—a zoo with a beautiful prospect. Being built on a small island, the seal and polar bear enclosures embraced the very ocean: unique in any menagerie in the world.

Twice in these early days seals escaped. One returned after only one night in the open sea, presumably finding it pleasanter having his fish handed to him than having to hunt them himself. The other one swam round, landed again and climbed to the summit of the island, where he startled a picnic party by demanding food from them.

We may smile at these attempts to convert the young to a better way of life. But it is a fact that this question of animals and morality, if in a rather different form, is today a burning one.

Do we now see, from the days of the authors of the bestiaries, the wheel turning full circle?

It has never been difficult for believers in God to see animals as a manifestation of His glory: indeed, they can hardly fail to do so. Though atheists cannot share this view, they can —and quite certainly great numbers of them do—feel a deep moral conern over mankind's attitude towards the beasts, and fully share in the worldwide demand (growing, thank God, to a clamour) that not another single species shall be allowed to become extinct.

Like so many wonderful things in life, it is only when you are in danger of losing them that you understand how truly precious they are.

In the last ten years, especially since the founding of the World Wildlife Fund in 1961, there has been tremendous advance in this kind of thinking, and happily in nearly all countries. People are aware, as perhaps never before, of how necessary wild animals are to us. Necessary in every way. Not simply for the delight we may have in their strangeness, beauty and grace: and that thousands do so appreciate them is borne out by the popularity of zoos, "safari" parks and (not so accessible, but drawing more and more people all the time) the huge wild nature reserves of Africa and other lands, where the animals may be seen in their free majesty. Important as this aesthetic side is, as is too the holding even, as far as is possible, that marvellous mystery known as the balance of nature, yet there is a deeper level.

We need the animals for our souls' sake. There *is* an affinity between us and the beasts, and we cannot, dare not break it. Heaven knows we have tortured, and do torture them, abuse them in every kind of way, even past human forgiveness... and yet... and yet most of us would not care to live without some animal or bird at our hearth.

You who read this may not believe in the Book of Genesis, in the story of the animals being brought by the Lord to Adam to be named. Well, suppose it is a myth. It is yet a myth interpreting a Truth. We need animals; we cannot be happy and whole without them. Could anyone (outside Communist China where, I believe, the experiment is to some extent being tried)—could anyone cheerfully face a world where nothing living moved but Man?

The difficulty today is to find enough space in the world for the wild animals. There is no solution to this unless we humans can reduce our numbers. We are increasing at a terrifying rate; and the preservation of wild life is by no means the only reason why we should endeavour with all our hearts and skill to do this.

This is necessarily a long term remedy. But to help to save the animals there is one thing that could be done rapidly. Only let every country ban the import of all wild furs. With that trade gone, one of the greatest temptations to killing animals vanishes overnight. Furs are no longer even necessary. A Polar expedition has worn simulated fur, and found themselves as warm as though clad in skins.

It is a new era too for zoos. In the past their functions were to provide amusement, education, study of natural history and, in certain cases, edification. Now they are as concerned as the rest of the world with conservation. Obviously it is desirable that every creature shall remain represented in a wild state, and this is the aim of all conservationists, Directors of zoos included. What the zoos can do—and are doing—is to endeavour to breed in captivity those creatures in danger of extinction; so that, if the worst happens, and human pressures drive all the specimens from the wild, at least this rare animal, perhaps the Arabian oryx, will not vanish utterly from the earth. True, it will then be but as a picked bunch of bluebells in a vase to the azure glory beneath the trees in an April wood. But the day might come at last when it could be re-introduced into its native terrain...

Finally, a thought to ponder.

From time immemorial it has been accepted by the human race that in all circumstances a man's life was to be put before any animal's. I speak generally, of Man against Nature. Of course, if a hungry fellow poached the great lord's deer, or even stole a sheep or cow, he was, until comparatively recently, put to death. But that was considered a different affair altogether. Very long ago Man as a species was in far greater danger than any animal. The beasts were there in abundance: Man was striving to survive. So the concept of our superior value is deep (and, mostly, rightly deep) in our consciousness.

Now the former situation is reversed. The human race proliferates over the earth, killing and laying waste all that gets in its way. And remember, to destroy the environment is to destroy also the animal that dwells there.

So I would say unequivocally that supposing it were to be the case that there were only a couple of pairs (or little more) of living tigers anywhere in the world, the life of a man who deliberately and for greed shot one of these is of far less value than the irreplaceable living jewel he has destroyed.

This goes for all the rare species. Man has to spell out the humiliating lesson that now it is not he who is unexpendable, but those creatures that he has made rare and that, for all his skills, he can never refashion. They are gone in this world, to eternity.

It is his bounden duty, even at this eleventh hour, to be Adam, to be Noah...

Bibliography

Histoire des Ménageries de l'Antiquité à nos Jours. Gustave Loisel (3 vols) 1912.

The Tower Menagerie. E. T. Bennett 1829.

Memoirs of the Tower of London. John Britton & E. W. Brayley 1830.

An Historical Description of the Tower of London and its Curiosities. Anon. 1789.

Old and New London. Walter Thornbury (n. d. 19th cent.).

Wild Animals in Captivity. A. D. Bartlett 1899.

Wild Animals. J. F. Nott 1886.

Centenary History of the Zoological Society of London. P. Chalmers Mitchell 1929.

A History of the Earth and Animated Nature. Oliver Goldsmith 1774.

Natural History. Buffon (Eng. trs. 1812).

The Mind of the Ancient World, A consideration of Pliny's Natural History. H. N. Wethered 1937.

Cortes and Montezuma. Maurice Collis 1954.

Five Letters 1519—1526. Hernando Cortes (trs. J. Bayard Morris).

The Travels of Marco Polo. trs. fm L. F. Benedetto by Prof. Aldo Ricci.

The Book of Beasts. T. H. White (trs. of Latin Bestiary of the 12th cent. "made and edited T. H. W." 1954).

Antapodosis, Relatio de Legatione Constantinopolitana (The Embassy to Constantinople). fm. The Works of Liudprand of Cremona, trs. F. A. Wright 1930.

Book for a Rainy Day. J. T. Smith. 1845

Socrates and the Beasts. Elena Quarelli (Eng. trs. 1960).

Man and Wildlife. C. A. W. Guggisberg 1970.

Those about to Die. Daniel Mannix 1960.

Index